Richard R. Hammar,
J.D., LL.M., CPA

Church Governance

What leaders must know to conduct legally sound church business.

Published by Christianity Today International
ChurchLawAndTax.com
ChurchLawAndTaxStore.com

Executive Editor: Jim Bolton
Editors: Matt Branaugh, Michelle Dowell
Design: Vasil Nazar
Cover photo: GettyImages.com

Contents

Foreword

Say the words "fiduciary duty" or "parliamentary procedure" at a dinner party, and you can count on blank stares followed by speedy efforts to change the subject. (Ask me how I know this.) In fact, there's a fair chance that you had a similar reaction when you saw the title of this book. We might as well be honest: Board structure, elections, membership requirements, minutes, and business meetings will never land on anyone's list of "most exciting topics to learn about this year."

Stating at the outset that this resource is not a "thriller" may seem unfair, especially since my job is to commend this book and its author. But stick with me. If we agree that interest in understanding matters of church governance is low, we can likely also agree that proper, thoughtful governance is lacking in many churches. There are exceptions, yes, but I'd be a rich woman if I had a dime for every church leader who has questioned the true necessity of taking a proper vote or actually having a quorum, or who has told me, "Our bylaws really need work. We'll get to that someday." And if we could research the source of these expressions, I suspect we would discover two underlying assumptions—that governance sloppiness is inconsequential and that governance rules are difficult to understand. I'm here to tell you neither of these thoughts is true, and this book is the proof.

First and foremost, you should know that *Church Governance: What Leaders Must Know to Conduct Legally Sound Church Business* is designed to tell you what you need to know, not to make you an expert. The book is organized as a ready-reference tool, with chapter and topic headings that will help you quickly find answers to commonly asked questions. And it is written in a style a lay person can understand. Richard Hammar, Michael Martin, and Frank and Elaine Sommerville are seasoned professionals and true experts. But they've done a superb job of distilling a complex topic to its essentials and conveying the information in accessible language. You do not need to worry that opening this book will land you in a world of complicated terms and information overload.

Second, this resource includes just the right amount of "here's why this matters" talk. Yes, you definitely should understand what might happen if you fail to follow the law or best practices, but the authors know their audience well, and they've wisely avoided trying to turn readers into accountants or lawyers. In short, there's enough here to help you appreciate the risks, spot potential issues, and know when to ask for help.

Leading any organization is weighty business. But leading a church brings unique responsibilities and burdens because the church is Christ's body. I know you want to care for that body well—and not just its individual parts, but the whole of it. Exploring this resource will allow you to take steps toward a better understanding of the role that proper governance plays in caring for the body of Christ. And as you do so, I know you'll find this book to be a trusted counselor and encouraging friend.

Sarah E. Merkle
Editorial advisor for Church Law & Tax
Attorney and professional parliamentarian
Bradley Arant Boult Cummings LLP

Church Incorporation

Why would a church want to incorporate? An important advantage to corporation status is that individual members cannot be personally liable for the debts and obligations of the church, or for the acts of other members.

What is incorporation?

Incorporation is a simple process by which an organization is recognized by the state as a legal entity. Two forms of church corporations are in widespread use in the United States. By far the more common form is the *membership corporation,* which is composed of and controlled by church members. Several states also recognize *trustee corporations.* The trustees of a trustee corporation constitute and control the corporation. A few states also permit certain officers of hierarchical churches to form a *corporation sole,* which is a corporation consisting of a single individual.

In a few states, churches historically were not permitted to incorporate. For example, the constitution of Virginia prohibited the issuance of a charter of incorporation to "any church or religious denomination." However, a federal court in 2002 ruled that the Virginia constitution's ban on church incorporation violated the first amendment guaranty of religious freedom.

How does a church become incorporated?

The Model Nonprofit Corporation Act, which has been adopted in whole or in part by several states, provides a uniform method of incorporation for several kinds of nonprofit organizations, including religious organizations (see "Highlights from the Model Nonprofit Corporation Act" at the end of this article). The procedure consists of the following steps: (1) preparation of duplicate articles of incorporation setting forth the corporation's name, period of duration, address of registered office within the state, name and address of a registered agent, purposes, and names and addresses of the initial board of directors and incorporators; (2) notarized signature of the duplicate articles of incorporation by the incorporators; and (3) submission of the prescribed filing fee and duplicate articles of incorporation to the secretary of state. The secretary of state reviews the articles of incorporation to ensure compliance with the Act. If the articles of incorporation are satisfactory, the secretary of state endorses both duplicate copies, files one in his or her office, and returns the other along with a certificate of incorporation to the church. The church's corporate existence begins at the moment the certificate of incorporation is issued. Many states have a special procedure for church incorporation that churches can elect in lieu of the general nonprofit corporation law.

How can you determine if your church is incorporated?

Unfortunately, many church board members do not know if their church is incorporated. You can quickly and easily check to see if your church is incorporated by contacting the office of the secretary of state in your state capital. Representatives of the office of secretary of state ordinarily will tell you over the telephone whether or not your church is incorporated, or you can search online through your secretary of state's website. If you are informed that your church is incorporated, then you may wish to ask for a certificate of good standing (the name of this document varies somewhat from state to state) that confirms the corporate status of your church. You also should request a certified copy of your charter (articles of incorporation), to be sure that you have a copy of the document on file with the state. Calling the office of the secretary of state is important even if you think that your church is incorporated, since the corporate status of many churches has "lapsed" through failure to file annual reports with the state. In many states, church corporations must file relatively simple annual reports with the office of secretary of state. Churches sometimes fail to file these reports. In some states, a failure to file an annual report will cause the church's corporate status to lapse.

Advantages of incorporation

In general, a church can either be a corporation or an unincorporated association. In the past, incorporation had a number of advantages over the unincorporated form of organization, including the following:

- a corporation, unlike an unincorporated association, can own or transfer property in its own name
- a corporation, unlike an unincorporated association, can enter into contracts or other legal obligations
- a corporation, unlike an unincorporated association, can sue or be sued
- the members of a corporation, unlike the members of an unincorporated association, are not personally liable for the acts of other members

In recent years, many states have enacted laws that treat unincorporated associations similarly to corporations, at least in some respects. In many states, unincorporated churches can own property in the church's name (instead of in the name of trustees), and they can enter into contracts and sue or be sued. In some states, these laws result in there being very little difference between incorporated and unincorporated churches.

The one advantage to corporation status is that it insures that individual members of a church cannot be personally liable for the debts and obligations of the church, or for the acts of other members. Of course, members can be personally liable for their own acts. But if a church is incorporated, a member cannot be personally liable for the acts of another member. To illustrate, assume that a member molests a child, and the child's parents sue the offender and the church. A jury awards $1 million in damages. The church has no insurance or assets to cover this award. Can other members be personally liable? Not if the church is incorporated, since incorporation insulates members from personal liability for the acts of other members.

It must be noted that very few attempts have been made by plaintiffs' attorneys to sue the members of unincorporated churches for damages resulting from the acts of other members. But it is also true that we live in the most litigious society on earth. It is inevitable that more plaintiffs will seek to sue the members of unincorporated churches in their efforts to find "deep pockets" to satisfy potential judgments. This problem will be aggravated by "gaps" in many churches' insurance policies. For example, many churches are not insured for sexual misconduct, or their coverage is limited, yet such claims can result in substantial court judgments. In such cases, it is possible that attorneys will check to see if the church is unincorporated (or if its corporate status has lapsed) to determine if individual members may be personally liable. There is a simple remedy for those wishing to avoid this personal liability (save for any criminal acts committed)—incorporation.

Disadvantages of incorporation

The only disadvantage to incorporation is cost. However, the cost of retaining an attorney to incorporate a church ordinarily is modest.

Some have argued that another disadvantage of incorporation is the increased "government regulation" that incorporation entails. It is true that the Model Nonprofit Corporation Act regulates virtually every aspect of corporate governance. But, the Act specifies that most of its provisions are applicable only if a corporation has not provided otherwise in its articles of incorporation or bylaws. Churches often are unwittingly controlled by the Act through their failure to adopt articles or bylaws dealing with particular issues of church governance that are addressed in the Act. Some churches of course consider this to be an advantage, for it means that there will be authoritative direction on most questions of church administration.

A few have maintained that churches should never incorporate since incorporation constitutes a "subordination" of a church to the authority of the state. Such a view reflects a fundamental misunderstanding regarding the legal status of corporations. A church that incorporates is subordinating merely the artificial corporate entity to the state, and it is free to terminate that entity at any time. The church remains free to dissolve its corporate status at any time, should it deem this necessary, without any effect on the real "church."

What is the Revised Model Nonprofit Corporation Act?

The Revised Model Nonprofit Corporation Act is influential in many states. But what is it? Here are some highlights to help church leaders better understand its history, purpose, and influence on governance-related matters:

- "No federal law governs nonprofit corporations or nonprofit organizations generally. Most states have nonprofit corporation laws, although some state corporation statutes apply to both for-profit and nonprofit corporations. . . . The Revised Model Nonprofit Corporation Act (1987) . . . serves as a guide for state bar associations and legislatures in drafting the various state statutes. While the availability of a model act provides some degree of uniformity, statutes vary significantly among states."

KEY POINT *Finding your state's nonprofit corporation act will require researching your state's statutes. Legal databases are one source for this information and qualified legal counsel can assist with research as well. The Harvard Law School Library also provides a free guide assisting with the researching of state laws: https://guides.library.harvard.edu/statutes. Lastly, books and resources published about state nonprofit corporation law, and publications like National Parliamentarian (published by the National Association of Parliamentarians), occasionally release a survey of nonprofit corporation laws by state.*

- "Many nonprofit organizations are exempt from taxation under federal and state laws. However, tax laws have nothing to do with an organization's status as a corporation or other entity. An organization becomes a corporation and is subject to state corporation laws only when it is incorporated under the law of some state. . . . Statutes and courts differentiate among the various types of nonprofit organizations and tend to categorize them according to their respective purposes and accomplishments."
- "A nonprofit corporation may provide its own governing rules and regulations, which will supersede statutory mandates in some cases. Notwithstanding the corporation's intent or characterization of its activities, a nonprofit corporation may not engage in activities prohibited by statute."
- The Revised Model Nonprofit Act speaks to a variety of important topics, including the fiduciary duties of directors to their organizations, stating "a director shall discharge his or her duties as a director in good faith, with the care that an ordinarily prudent person in a like position would exercise under

> similar circumstances, and in a manner the director reasonably believes to be in the best interests of the corporation." The Act also addresses issues ranging from conflicts of interest to derivative actions.
>
> — Source: **William E. Knepper**, et al., *Liability of Corporate Officers and Directors* (November 2017)

Church Bylaws

A church's bylaws are the main rules that govern how the church is run, so it is essential that every board member is familiar with them.

Most churches, whether incorporated or unincorporated, have a governing document that addresses several issues of governance and administration. While the name for this document varies from church to church, it often is called *bylaws*, and it is this name that will be used in this article as a matter of convenience.

Bylaws are self-imposed rules, resulting from an agreement or contract between the corporation and its members to conduct the corporate business in a particular way.

What are bylaws?

The Model Nonprofit Corporations Act (3rd ed. 2008), which has been adopted by several states, defines bylaws as "the code or codes of rules (other than the articles of incorporation) adopted for the regulation and governance of the internal affairs of the nonprofit corporation, regardless of the name or names used to refer to those rules."

One court defined bylaws as follows:

> The bylaws of a corporation are the rules of law for its government. The term "bylaw" may be further defined according to its function, which is to prescribe the rights and duties of the members with reference to the internal government of the corporation, the management of its affairs, and the rights and duties existing among the members. Bylaws are self-imposed rules, resulting from an agreement or contract between the corporation and its members to conduct the corporate business in a particular way. Until repealed, bylaws are the continuing rule for the government of the corporation and its officers. *Schraft v. Leis, 686 P.2d 865 (Kan. 1984)*.

Because bylaws contain rules for internal governance and administration, they are indispensable for both incorporated and unincorporated churches.

Know your current version

In many churches, the bylaws were adopted long ago, and have been amended numerous times over the years. As a result, there may be various "editions" in circulation. Often, these editions are undated, and this can make it difficult if not impossible to identify the current one. This can create confusion.

EXAMPLE

A church conducts an annual business meeting at which 15 percent of the members are present. Some members question whether a quorum exists. Church staff scour the church office, looking for a copy of the church's bylaws. Two editions are found. One defines a quorum as 20 percent of the church's membership, and the second defines a quorum as 10 percent of the church's membership. Neither edition is dated, and no one knows which of these editions is more recent, or even if either of them represents the current edition. What steps can church leaders take to identify the current version of the church bylaws? Two common procedures that can be very effective in identifying the current edition of a church's bylaws:

- Identify copies of the church bylaws with a numeric designation. To illustrate, a church identifies its current bylaws as "version 1.0." During the church's membership meeting in 2010, two amendments are made to the bylaws. Following the meeting, the revised bylaws are printed, and designated as "version 1.1."
- Identify copies of the church bylaws by date. For example, designate the current bylaws "Current as of [date]." Leaders can also reference church minutes for help in determining the proper version.

In either case, be sure that all printed copies of the bylaws bear the appropriate designation, and dispose of undesignated versions.

Constitution and bylaws

Some churches have both a constitution and bylaws. But there is little justification for a church to have both a constitution and bylaws unless the constitution is made superior to the bylaws either by express provision or by a more restrictive amendment procedure.

Identifying a single body of rules as the "constitution and bylaws" without any attempt to distinguish between the two is a common but inappropriate practice.

To illustrate, some churches have (1) a constitution that can only be amended by providing members with advance notice of the proposed amendment prior to a membership meeting, and by a two-thirds vote of the membership at the meeting; and (2) bylaws that can be amended at a membership meeting, without prior notice to the members, and by a simple majority vote. The church places provisions of greatest importance in the constitution, such as church doctrine and the purchase or sale of church assets, since these can be changed only through a more deliberative process involving advance notice and a super-majority vote. Routine provisions are assigned to the bylaws.

Churches that have both a constitution and bylaws typically address many of the same issues in both documents. Over time, this often leads to conflicts, since amendments in one document may not be made to similar provisions in the other.

What to include in the bylaws

The *Model Nonprofit Corporations Act (3rd ed. 2008),* which has been adopted by several states, states that "the bylaws of a nonprofit corporation may contain any provision for managing the activities and regulating the affairs of the corporation that is not inconsistent with law or the articles of incorporation." The following subjects generally pertain to "managing the activities and regulating the affairs of" a church, and are commonly included in a church's bylaws:

- Qualifications, selection, discipline, and removal of members.
- Time and place of annual business meetings.
- The calling of special business meetings.
- Notice for regular and special meetings.
- Quorums at meetings of the membership and church board.
- Voting rights and requirements.
- Selection, tenure, and removal of officers and directors.
- Filing of vacancies on the church board.
- Responsibilities of directors (deacons, elders) and officers.
- The procedure for amending bylaws.

- The procedure and voting requirements for purchases and conveyances of church property.
- The designation of standing committees (such as audit committee, an investment committee, and an insurance committee).
- Dissolution procedures.

The drafting or amending of church bylaws is a complex task that should not be attempted without the assistance of an attorney. Knowing what to include, and exclude, from your bylaws are important tasks that require legal knowledge and experience.

Helpful provisions to include in your bylaws

There are a number of potentially helpful provisions that are often omitted from church bylaws. These include the following:

- An arbitration or mediation provision requiring specified disputes to be resolved through mediation or binding arbitration.
- Choice of parliamentary law to govern membership meetings. Many church leaders assume that *Robert's Rules of Order Newly Revised* governs church business meetings. But there are dozens of competing manuals of parliamentary procedure, and a church should formally select the model that will be applied. If your church intends to use *Robert's Rules of Order Newly Revised,* then your bylaws should say so.
- If your church bylaws contain a provision addressing the discipline of members who violate your standards of membership, it should clarify that members who have been charged with conduct in violation of the standards of membership waive their right to resign from membership in the church. Without such a provision, members can preempt a church's disciplinary procedure by simply informing their pastor that they are resigning as members.

- A clause specifying how contracts and other legal documents are to be approved.
- Who has the authority to sign church checks? It is a basic tenet of internal control that two persons sign checks, and a church's bylaws should specify which two officers have this authority.
- "Bonding" of officers and employees who handle church funds.
- An annual audit by independent certified public accountants. There are compelling reasons why a church should consider having an annual audit. Most importantly, an audit promotes an environment of accountability in which opportunities for embezzlement (and therefore the risk of embezzlement) are reduced. And, the CPAs who conduct the audit will provide the church leadership with a "management letter" that points out weaknesses and inefficiencies in the church's accounting and financial procedures. This information can be invaluable to church leaders. Smaller churches that cannot afford a full audit may want to consider two other options: (1) Hire a CPA to conduct a review, which is a simpler and less expensive procedure. If the review detects irregularities, a full audit may be considered worth the price. (2) Create an internal audit committee if there are accountants or business leaders within the church who have the ability to review accounting procedures and practices and look for weaknesses. These people often are very familiar with sound internal control policies, and will quickly correct weaknesses in the church's financial operations.
- An indemnification clause providing for the indemnification of officers and directors who are sued as a result of actions or decisions made in the course of performing their duties on behalf of the church.
- Specification of the church's fiscal year.
- "Staggered election" of directors (a portion of the board is elected

each year to ensure year-to-year continuity of leadership).

- The bylaws should specify if the church board can act without conducting a formal meeting. To illustrate, section 8.21 of the Model Nonprofit Corporation Bylaws, which has been adopted by several states, specifies that "except to the extent that the articles of incorporation or bylaws require that action by the board of directors be taken at a meeting, action required or permitted to be taken by the board of directors may be taken without a meeting if each director signs a consent in the form of a record describing the action to be taken and delivers it to the nonprofit corporation. ... A consent signed under this section has the effect of action taken at a meeting of the board of directors and may be described as such in any document."
- The bylaws should authorize the church board to conduct meetings by telephone, or allow the "attendance" of an otherwise absent director through telephone connection, if desired.
- The bylaws should specify if absentee voting is permitted at membership meetings. Absentee voting is not ordinarily permitted unless expressly authorized by an organization's bylaws.
- The bylaws should specify if proxy voting is permitted at membership meetings.
- Who is authorized to have custody of the minutes of church membership and board meetings?
- Who is authorized to have custody of the church's financial records? These documents are church records, and ordinarily should not be entrusted to the treasurer's personal possession.
- Most state nonprofit corporation laws give members a right to inspect specified corporate records at a proper time and for a proper purpose. Usually, these laws provide that this authority

to inspect corporate records exists unless limited or abolished by the corporate bylaws. To illustrate, the Revised Model Nonprofit Corporation Act, which has been enacted by several states, gives members a right to inspect the minutes of board meetings if the member's demand is made in good faith and for a proper purpose; the member describes with "reasonable particularity" the purpose and the records the member desires to inspect; and the records are directly connected with this purpose. The Act specifies that a church's articles of incorporation or bylaws "may limit or abolish the right of a member under this section to inspect and copy any corporate record."

- Clarify the meaning of all voting requirements specified in the bylaws. For example, a church's bylaws may call for a "two-thirds vote" for certain actions. This can have various meanings, including a vote that is precisely two-thirds of the membership; at least two-thirds of the total voting membership, regardless of how many come to a business meeting; or, at least two-thirds of the members present at a duly called meeting at which a quorum is present. This kind of ambiguity has caused countless internal church disputes. Another common option is a majority of those present and voting.

- Suspension or removal of board members who miss a specified number of board meetings. Board members owe various "fiduciary duties" to their church, and one of these is the duty to exercise "due care" in the performance of their responsibilities. Board members who miss most board meetings eventually will be in violation of this duty, and some churches have chosen to address this issue in their bylaws with a provision calling for the suspension or removal of such persons. The fiduciary duty of due care goes to the very heart of the status of a board member.

- Conflict of interest policy. In 2008, the IRS ruled that a nonprofit corporation did not qualify as a tax exempt church, in part because its governing document did not have a conflict of interest policy. The IRS noted that to qualify for exemption, an organization must be operated for public rather than private purposes, and "the organization has the burden of demonstrating this by showing that it is not operated for the benefit of private individuals, such as its creator and his family." The IRS concluded: "You have not adopted bylaws or provided specific information about the governance of your organization, nor have you adopted a conflict of interest policy .... The structure of your organization indicates that it can be used to benefit private individuals, such as [the founder] and his family, and you lack safeguards that would help to prevent such use." *IRS Letter Ruling 200830028.* This ruling is significant because of the importance the IRS assigned to a conflict of interest policy despite the fact that neither the tax code nor regulations specifically require that a church have such a policy. The IRS concluded that the lack of a conflict of interest policy tends to show that a family-governed entity is operated for private rather than public interests and is therefore ineligible for exemption. While this concern will not directly apply to most churches, it is a point worth considering with the attorney who drafts or reviews your church's bylaws.

- It is common for church board members to resign their position when they relocate or become incapacitated. However, church bylaws usually do not address when and how such resignations will occur. This is an important and frequently overlooked issue, since board members generally remain liable for the actions of the board until their resignation is effective. If the timing of a resignation is ambiguous, then this can create lingering exposure to liability. To avoid this, a church's bylaws should clarify precisely how and when a board member's resignation will be effective.

What not to include in a church's bylaws

Matters not related to the internal governance and administration of a church are more appropriately addressed elsewhere, such as in resolutions or policies. One of the reasons for addressing some items in resolutions and policies is that they can be amended more easily than waiting for the next regular business meeting to amend the bylaws, or calling a special one.

Examples of such items include:

- Personnel policies for church employees, addressing such items as compensation, benefits, religious preferences, discipline and terminations, sexual harassment, and employment standards. These matters are best addressed in a written policy.
- Rules for the selection and supervision of volunteers who will work with minors are best addressed in a written policy.
- Some churches that define marriage as a union between a man and a woman have amended their bylaws to include a statement to this effect. In many cases, this is unnecessary, since the church's position on marriage can be established through other provisions in its bylaws (i.e., a provision making the Bible the final authority on all matters of doctrine and conduct), and through its established practice.
- The bylaws of an incorporated church need not include items that are required to be included in the articles of incorporation (see below).

Articles of incorporation

The application for incorporation that is filed with the secretary of state generally is called the *articles of incorporation* or *articles of agreement.* This document, when approved and certified by the appropriate government official, is commonly referred to as the corporate charter. Church charters typically set forth the following information:

- corporate name
- corporate address
- period of duration
- purposes of the corporation
- names and addresses of incorporators and directors

In addition, the income tax regulations require that the assets of a church pass to another tax-exempt organization upon its dissolution. The IRS has stated that the following paragraph will satisfy this requirement if contained in a church corporation's articles of incorporation:

> Upon the dissolution of the corporation, assets shall be distributed for one or more exempt purposes within the meaning of section 501(c)(3) of the Internal Revenue Code, or the corresponding section of any future federal tax code, or shall be distributed to the federal government, or to a state or local government, for a public purpose. Any such assets not so disposed of shall be disposed of by a Court of Competent Jurisdiction of the county in which the principal office of the corporation is then located, exclusively for such purposes or to such organization or organizations, as said Court shall determine, which are organized and operated exclusively for such purposes.

Most churches prefer to specify the religious organization to which their assets will be distributed in the event of dissolution rather than leaving this determination to a judge's discretion. There is no assurance, under the suggested IRS language, that a dissolved church's assets would even go to another religious organization. For example, a judge could transfer a dissolved church's assets to a city or state government, or to a non-religious charitable organization, under the IRS language. Of course, churches wishing to designate a religious organization in their dissolution clauses should condition the distribution upon that organization's existence and tax-exempt status at the time of the distribution.

The IRS Internal Revenue Manual and IRS Publication 557 both require that an appropriate dissolution clause appear in a church's articles of incorporation. However, the IRS has conceded that no dissolution clause is required if state law requires that the assets of a dissolved church corporation (or other charitable corporation) be distributed to another tax-exempt organization. The instructions to IRS Form 1023 (Application for Recognition of Exemption) state that "if you are a corporation formed in the following states, then you do not need a specific provision in your articles of incorporation providing for the distribution of assets upon dissolution: Arkansas, California, Louisiana, Massachusetts, Minnesota, Missouri, Ohio, Oklahoma."

The IRS also suggests that the following two paragraphs be placed in a church corporation's articles of incorporation:

> Said corporation is organized exclusively for charitable, religious, educational, and scientific purposes, including, for such purposes, the making of distributions to organizations that qualify as exempt organizations under section 501(c)(3) of the Internal Revenue Code, or the corresponding section of any future federal tax code.
>
> No part of the net earnings of the corporation shall inure to the benefit of, or be distributable to its members, trustees, officers, or other private persons, except that the corporation shall be authorized and empowered to pay reasonable compensation for services rendered and to make payments and distributions in furtherance of the purposes set forth in Article Third hereof. No substantial part of the activities of the corporation shall be the carrying on of propaganda, or otherwise attempting to influence legislation, and the corporation shall not participate in, or intervene in (including

> the publishing or distribution of statements) any political campaign on behalf of or in opposition to any candidate for public office. Notwithstanding any other provision of these articles, the corporation shall not carry on any other activities not permitted to be carried on (a) by a corporation exempt from federal income tax under section 501(c)(3) of the Internal Revenue Code, or the corresponding section of any future federal tax code, or (b) by a corporation, contributions to which are deductible under section 170(c)(2) of the Internal Revenue Code, or the corresponding section of any future federal tax code.

If reference to federal law in articles of incorporation imposes a limitation that is invalid in your state, you may wish to substitute the following for the last sentence of the preceding paragraph:

> Notwithstanding any other provision of these articles, this corporation shall not, except to an insubstantial degree, engage in any activities or exercise any powers that are not in furtherance of the purposes of this corporation.

KEY POINT *Some churches define their exempt purposes to include charity and education in addition to religion, believing that this will accommodate a greater diversity of ministries. However, note that such an expansion of corporate purposes may also jeopardize various exemptions that are available to "religious" organizations. Church leaders should discuss this important issue with an attorney.*

[See Table 1 in Appendix: Provisions Commonly Found in Governing Documents]

Resolutions

Corporate resolutions are not bylaws. A resolution is an informal and temporary enactment for disposing of a particular item of business. Bylaws are rules of general applicability. For example, a minister's housing allowance generally is designated by the church board in a resolution. Similarly, a church's business expense reimbursement policy or medical insurance reimbursement plan ordinarily appears in resolutions of the church board.

Ambiguous terminology

Church bylaws often contain ambiguous language, and this can result in both confusion and internal disputes. It is essential for church bylaws to be reviewed periodically by the board, or a special committee, to identify ambiguities and propose modifications. Will the civil courts interfere in a church dispute over the meaning of ambiguous bylaw provisions? Generally, the civil courts have been willing to do so if no interpretation of doctrine is required.

Reconciling conflicting provisions

Occasionally, conflicts develop among provisions in a corporation's charter, constitution, bylaws, and resolutions. The general rule is that provisions in a corporate charter take precedence over conflicting provisions in a corporation's constitution, bylaws, or resolutions.

Rules of construction

Several courts have ruled that bylaws are to be construed according to the same rules that apply to contracts. A leading treatise on contract law, *Fletcher, Cyclopedia of the Law of Corporations § 4195,* summarizes the rules of construction as follows:

> Words of corporate bylaws are to be interpreted in their ordinary, popular sense .... A bylaw will be construed in harmony with the

charter if it is reasonably possible to do so. Additionally, a bylaw will be interpreted to avoid conflicts among its provisions. In the interpretation of bylaw provisions, courts must give effect to the intent of the parties as revealed by the language of the bylaws and the circumstances surrounding their creation and adoption. The intent of the [drafters] in enacting particular bylaw amendments is instructive in determining whether any ambiguity exists. A construction that will render a bylaw just and equal in its operation will be adopted in preference to one that will have a contrary effect. Another principle of construction adopted by some courts is that no provision of a bylaw should unnecessarily be rendered meaningless or superfluous. The rules used to interpret statutes, contracts, and other written instruments are applicable when construing corporate bylaws ....

If a bylaw is unambiguous in its language, a court will not interpret it or search for the parties' intent behind the bylaw. But where there exist reasonable and contradictory interpretations of a bylaw provision, its interpretation is a question or fact for the jury, reviewable by a court for clear error. A bylaw is not made ambiguous merely because parties disagree on its proper construction; in order to be ambiguous the bylaw must be reasonably susceptible of different constructions or interpretations. However, ambiguity may be found when the bylaw is read together with another corporate document. The contract is to be construed against the party who drafted it when the surrounding circumstances do not clarify the ambiguity.

Ambiguous or obscure provisions should be construed to make them harmonize with the general intent of the bylaws as a whole, and to promote the business welfare of the corporation. ... In determining the rights of a member of a corporation under its bylaws, portions dealing with the same subject must also be construed. If it can be ascertained, the design and intent of the framers of the bylaw must prevail, and where a particular bylaw was adopted to meet a specific situation, the purpose for which it was adopted is pertinent in determining the proper construction to be given it.

Amendment procedures

Most bylaws provide for their own amendment, and it is important for church leaders to be familiar with this procedure to ensure that amendments are handled correctly. Consider the following points:

- Some church bylaws permit amendments to occur at any membership meeting, without advance notice to members.
- Some church bylaws require that members be notified a specified number of days in advance of a membership meeting at which a bylaw amendment will be considered. If advance notice is required, then a failure to comply with this requirement will jeopardize the legal validity of any amendments that occur, no matter how many members support the amendments.
- In some cases, church leaders decide not to wait until the next annual business meeting to present a proposed bylaw amendment to the congregation, and a special business meeting is called. However, note that state nonprofit corporation law generally requires that the notice provided to members of the date, time, and place of a special business meeting also state the purpose for which the meeting is being called. If the notice to members fails to specify that an amendment to the bylaws will be considered, including the text of the proposed amendment that will be presented during the meeting, then the legal validity of such an amendment will be jeopardized.
- Some church bylaws require a super majority (i.e., greater than a simple majority) to amend certain provisions. For example, an amendment to church doctrine, or to the requirements for the sale or acquisition of church property, often require a two-thirds or even

a three-fourths vote. Church leaders must be familiar with the voting requirement that will apply to any proposed bylaw amendment.

Is it time to rewrite our bylaws?

Do church bylaws ever need to be rewritten? That depends on several factors, including the following:

- How old are the bylaws? The older they are, the more likely they are in need of a legal review, and possibly revisions or a new and updated document.
- Who drafted the bylaws? If the bylaws were drafted by one or more attorneys with experience in corporate governance, ideally involving churches or other nonprofit organizations, there is less need to rewrite the bylaws. On the other hand, many churches have bylaws that were drafted by a committee of laypersons with little if any specialized knowledge in corporate governance. In such a case, there may be a greater need for revisions or a new document.
- Some church bylaws are mandated by the denomination with which they are affiliated, and the church has little if any authority to make any changes. Church leaders should be familiar with any such limitations.

Do we need to file our bylaws with the state?

Unincorporated churches generally are not required to file bylaws with the state. But there may be exceptions, depending on state law. For example, an unincorporated church may need to submit a copy of its bylaws to a state agency to demonstrate entitlement to a property or sales tax exemption or a preferential zoning classification. In many states, incorporated churches are not required to file their bylaws with the state corporation commission as part of the incorporation process. Check with your state's corporation commission to be sure. As is the case with unincorporated churches, an incorporated church may need to submit a copy of its bylaws to a state agency for various reasons, such as to demonstrate entitlement to a property or sales tax exemption or a preferential zoning classification.

The application of denominational governing documents

In many denominations, affiliated churches are limited in their ability to compose or revise their bylaws. In some cases, the church's bylaws are entirely prescribed by the denomination's governing document. In others, the church is free to compose its own bylaws, but must include terms mandated by the denomination's governing document. As one court noted, "For religious nonprofit corporations, bylaws may partly be prescribed by, and may be an important tie to, a related superior or affiliated religious organization." *New v. Kroeger, 84 Cal.Rptr.3d 464 (Cal. App. 2008).*

Church Documents and Records

A review of the important documents and records used to run the church business that every board member should be familiar with.

Articles of Incorporation (or Charter)

If your church is incorporated, the document that you submitted to a court or to the secretary of state to become incorporated is generally referred to as the articles of incorporation. It is typically a short document that contains the church's name, address, period of duration, initial board of directors, and statement of purposes. When this document is recognized by the state, and the church's corporate status begins, the articles of incorporation is called the charter. There are a few things that church board members should know about their church charter.

First, it is the most authoritative legal document that the church has. In the event of a conflict between the charter and any other legal document, the charter generally will control.

Second, since the charter defines the purposes for which your church was established, it is important for you to be familiar with this document.

Third, the charter may contain restrictions or limitations that the board needs to be aware of. For example, some charters impose restrictions on the sale or purchase of church property, the size of the board, and debt limits. Others contain a reverter or dissolution clause specifying what happens to the church's property if certain conditions occur.

Fourth, the IRS requires that certain provisions be included in a church's charter. These include prohibitions on political activities and the payment of unreasonable compensation. It would be well to review your charter to be sure this language is included.

Fifth, you should also check the period of duration specified in your church charter. This provision will determine the length of your church's corporate life. Many churches were incorporated years ago for a specific number of years. In some cases this period expires without anyone knowing about it. The result is that the corporate status of the church lapses.

Unfortunately, this can have negative consequences, since it may expose church members to personal liability. So, be sure to review your charter and determine the period of duration of your church. It should say perpetual. If not, you may want to consider amending your charter. Also, be sure you are familiar with your charter's statement of purpose.

The church constitution or bylaws

This is the document that contains most of a church's rules of internal administration and governance. While the name for this document varies from church to church, I will refer to it simply as a church's bylaws.

At a minimum, church bylaws should cover

- the qualifications, selection, and expulsion of members;
- the time and place of your annual business meetings;
- the calling of special business meetings;

- notice for annual and special meetings;
- quorums;
- voting rights;
- selection, tenure, and removal of officers and directors;
- filling of vacancies on the church board;

Many churches have bylaw provisions that call for the periodic review of the membership list to be sure that it is up to date. Do your church bylaws contain such a provision?

- responsibilities of directors and officers;
- the method of amending the bylaws;
- the purchase and conveyance of property.

Other matters that should be considered for inclusion in church bylaws include:

- the adoption of a specific manual of parliamentary procedure;
- a clause requiring certain disputes between church members, or between a member and the church itself, to be resolved through mediation or binding arbitration;
- a clause specifying how contracts and other legal documents are to be approved and signed;
- signature authority on checks;
- "bonding" of officers and employees who handle church funds;
- an annual audit by independent certified public accountants;
- an indemnification clause;
- specification of the church's fiscal year;

- "staggered voting" of board members—meaning that a portion of the board is elected each year to ensure year-to-year continuity of leadership.

It is essential for church board members to be familiar with their church's bylaws, since this document covers so many issues of church governance. (If you have not read your church bylaws, I urge you to do so.) Church bylaws often contain ambiguous language, and this is a major source of church disputes. For this reason, among others, it is a good practice to have your bylaws reviewed periodically by a local attorney. One final point concerning church bylaws: it is a good practice to date your bylaws. This will avoid the common problem of a church having multiple versions of bylaws with no clear idea of which is the most recent.

Church accounting and financial records

These records obviously come in a variety of formats. Church board members owe various fiduciary duties to their church, and these include familiarity with the church's financial records. It is your responsibility to insure that appropriate safeguards are implemented with regard to the handling of contributions, that cash and expenses are properly recorded and presented in the church's financial statements, and that the church is properly receipting donors for their contributions. You should be reviewing the finances of the church at each board meeting, and asking questions about anything that you don't understand or that seems irregular.

Current list of active voting members

It is often critical for a church to be able to identify those persons who are active voting members, since in most cases, important questions of church administration ultimately are decided by the members. For example, members often are empowered to elect pastors, or purchase or sell church property. Many churches have bylaw provisions that call for the periodic review of the membership list to be sure that it is up to date. Do your church bylaws contain such a provision? How recently did you review and update your membership list? Are you familiar with the procedure and grounds for removing members from this list? As a board member, you should be able to answer these questions.

Complete set of minutes of congregational meetings

Most churches conduct an annual business meeting, and occasionally hold quarterly and special meetings. Your church should keep minutes of all of these meetings. Churches should also maintain a complete set of minutes of board and committee meetings.

Copy of all insurance policies

Do you know where your church's general liability policy is maintained? Are you familiar with the terms of your policy? For example, do you know how much coverage your policy provides for personal injuries? What about incidents of sexual misconduct? Unfortunately, coverage for such incidents is reduced under some insurance policies, and it is essential for board members to know how much coverage their church has. If it is limited, then you either should be looking for additional coverage, or taking aggressive steps to adequately screen and supervise those persons who may have unsupervised access to children.

The Model Nonprofit Corporation Act, under which many churches are incorporated, requires incorporated churches to maintain complete books and records of account, minutes of business meetings, minutes of board meetings, and a listing of current members.

Complete set of tax records

These will include payroll tax forms, housing allowance designations for your pastors, contribution records, and any other forms you have filed with the federal government or with your state or local government. For example, you may have records to confirm your church's exemption from property taxes, or from state sales tax.

Full set of all corporate annual reports

These are the reports that your church filed with the secretary of state's office. In many states, incorporated churches are required to file an annual report with the secretary of state. This is a simple form that takes only a few minutes to complete. Failure to comply with this requirement can jeopardize a church's corporate status, thereby exposing church members and board members to personal liability. Church board members should know if their church is incorporated, if it is required to file annual reports with the secretary of state, and if it has consistently done so. If you are not sure, contact a local attorney, or call the secretary of state's office in your state capitol. In many states, this information is now available on a website maintained by the office of secretary of state.

Full set of employment records

These will include applications for employment, reference checks, information concerning disciplinary actions, the I-9 immigration form that all employers, including churches, must maintain for each new employee, and any other document relating to your employees.

Property deed

Have you seen this document? It may contain information of vital importance to your church. Let me give you an example. Many church deeds contain restrictions on the sale of the church's property. A common example is a donor who gives property to a church with a stipulation that it will belong to the church so long as it is used for church purposes. Many years later the church decides to sell the property and relocate, and only then does the church discover the restriction. The point is this: long before you consider selling your property, be sure to review your deed to see if there are any such restrictions that will limit the church's right to sell. A failure to do so may result in a reversion of the property back to the previous owner. Some of these records may be required by law. For example, the Model Nonprofit Corporation Act, under which many churches are incorporated, requires incorporated churches to maintain complete books and records of account, minutes of business meetings, minutes of board meetings, and a listing of current members. Most of a church's records are not required by law, but it is very important for board members to be able to identify and understand the relevant provisions in all of these records.

Four ways a church's documents could be opened for review

Church members have no inherent right to inspect church records. Such a right must be granted by some statute or legal document. Here are four ways this can occur:

1. *Your church is incorporated.* If a church is incorporated, then your state nonprofit corporation law may permit members to inspect records in some situations. Be sure that you research the correct statute, since in some states there is more than one corporation law under which a church can incorporate. Your charter often will identify the specific law under which the church was incorporated. The Model Nonprofit Corporation Act, which has been adopted in most states, gives members of an incorporated church the right to inspect corporate records for any proper purpose at any reasonable time. The Act defines records as books and records of account, minutes of business meetings, minutes of board meetings, and a listing of current members. There are a number of things to note about this provision: it applies only to incorporated churches; it applies only to members (persons who are not members of a church are given no right of inspection under this provision); the

right of inspection must be exercised at a reasonable time; and the right of inspection only applies if a member has a proper purpose in wanting to inspect church records. Parliamentary authority, including *Robert's Rules of Order (11th ed. 2011)*, also address inspection rights.

2. *Your church's charter.* A second legal basis for a right to inspect church records is the church's own charter or bylaws. Occasionally, these documents will contain a provision addressing the inspection of church records, and so they should be consulted.

3. *State securities law.* If your church issues securities, such as bonds or promissory notes, then state securities law will give investors, whether members or not, the right to inspect the financial records of the church.

4. *A subpoena.* A member may gain the legal right to inspect church records with a subpoena. Members and nonmembers alike may compel the disclosure or inspection of church records as part of a lawsuit against a church if the materials to be disclosed or inspected are relevant and not privileged. Under rules that have been adopted by most states and all federal courts, any party to a lawsuit may inspect records in the possession of another party to the lawsuit, and a party has the right, by a subpoena, to compel another party to turn over books, papers, and documents. Church leaders often are confused about their duty to comply with a subpoena that asks the church to turn over certain records as part of a lawsuit. For example, let's say that a church is sued by a former employee who claims that she was wrongfully dismissed. The church receives a subpoena demanding that it turn over a wide range of documents pertaining to its personnel practices, employees, and finances. Does the church have to respond to such a subpoena? Does the First Amendment guaranty of religious freedom somehow insulate it from having to respond? The answer is that church records are not inherently privileged or immune from the

subpoena power. Although all states consider confidential communications to be privileged when they are made to a minister acting in a professional capacity as a spiritual adviser, many courts have ruled that this privilege does not apply to church records.

There are two additional points to note about the inspection of church records. First, many church members have claimed that they have a right under the Privacy Act or the Freedom of Information Act to inspect church records. This is not the case. These laws apply to records maintained by the government, and not churches. Second, most courts have ruled that the First Amendment guaranty of religious freedom does not insulate church records from inspection by members. Churches should not assume that the First Amendment permits them to deny inspection rights given to members under state law.

Confidentiality of records

Churches accumulate a variety of documents and records, and some are confidential. Examples would be members' contributions records, counseling notes taken by a pastor or church counselor, references that you obtain when screening youth workers, or the minutes of board meetings at which sensitive issues are discussed. In any of these cases, the church faces possible legal liability if it permits disclosure of this information. As a result, it's important for church board members to take steps to insure that confidential information is not leaked or disclosed. There are a number of ways this can be done, and often this is simply a matter of recognizing the problem and using common sense. Here are a few precautions that some churches have taken to address this problem:

Keep confidential information in a locked file, preferably fireproof, and give the keys to a designated person, such as the treasurer or senior pastor, depending on the nature of the records involved. Some confidential information is stored on church computers, and steps must be taken to restrict access to this data by unauthorized persons. Confidential information should not be disclosed to persons without a legitimate need to know. For example, if the board dismisses a staff member due to a confession of misconduct, the pastor and board need to recognize that a public disclosure of this information can result in legal liability. The church board should consider adopting a covenant of confidentiality each year. Such a covenant is a written document, agreed to by the entire board, in which the board members covenant and agree not to disclose any confidential information shared during board meetings without the unanimous consent of the full board.

This kind of covenant helps to impress upon the board the highly confidential nature of some information, and reduces the legal risk to the church in the event that a board member violates the covenant and discloses confidential information. Of course, it won't work unless there is unanimous consent to it, so if one or more board members refuse to sign, they must be excused during any discussion of confidential information.

Finally, pastors often maintain counseling notes or other highly confidential records, and steps must be taken to insure the proper disposition of this information in the event of the sudden death or incapacity of the pastor.

How long should church records be retained?

Churches often wonder how long they need to keep or retain records. For example, how long should a church keep contribution records, tax forms, employment applications, screening forms, references, insurance policies, minutes, or correspondence? Unfortunately, there is no simple answer to these questions because a number of legal and practical considerations apply. What is needed is a records retention policy based on legal considerations and your church's needs that will make records retention decisions systematic and rational. Here are a few points that you may find helpful in developing a records retention policy in your church:

First, keep in mind that there are many reasons to keep church records. These include legal requirements under state or federal law, possible relevance in future litigation, the needs of the church, and historical importance. Second, make an inventory of existing records. Even when the period you have set for keeping a particular record has expired, do not automatically destroy it. You still may want to retain the document because of possible future litigation, or for historical purposes.

Some churches maintain a "destruction of records journal." When the period of time for keeping a record has expired, the record is described in the journal before being destroyed.

What is needed is a records retention policy based on legal considerations and your church's needs that will make records retention decisions systematic and rational.

But how long should a church retain records? There are some records that should be kept permanently. These include insurance policies, as well as screening forms and references. Insurance policies should be kept permanently because you will need them to establish what insurance company has a legal obligation to defend you in the event of an injury or loss occurring during the term of the insurance contract. This becomes important in cases of sexual misconduct, since many courts have greatly expanded the period of time during which a victim can file a lawsuit.

It is not uncommon today for churches to be sued for incidents of sexual misconduct that occurred years or even decades in the past. For example, let's say that your church is sued later this year for an alleged incident of child abuse that occurred 25 years ago. Would you know who your insurance carrier was in that year? Could you prove it by producing your insurance policy? If so, then a legal defense may be provided, and the insurance company will be responsible to pay any judgment or settlement up to the insurance limits. On the other hand, if you cannot produce your insurance policy from 25 years ago, and have no idea who your insurance carrier was that year, you probably will have to pay for your own legal defense and you will be responsible to pay any judgment or settlement. As you can see, it is absolutely essential for your church to retain all insurance policies.

Screening forms and references are another category of record that should be kept permanently—for the same reasons as insurance policies. You may need them in the event of litigation occurring many years in the future. If your church is sued because of an alleged failure to adequately screen workers, then you will need to be able to demonstrate the procedures you followed. This may be necessary many years, and in some cases decades, after you hired or selected the worker.

Many kinds of corporate records should also be kept permanently. These include your corporate charter, bylaws, minutes of congregational and board meetings, and any annual corporate reports that you file with the secretary of state. Some tax records should be kept permanently, and these include any forms relating to your exemption from federal or state taxes.

Any document that you plan to keep permanently should be stored in a secure location. This means a locked and fireproof file cabinet, or some other suitable location. Copies should be retained in another location.

There are a few kinds of tax records that a church should keep permanently. Most church records, however, don't need to be stored permanently. The IRS Tax Guide for Churches recommends that churches retain payroll tax forms for at least four years after filing the return. These include Forms W-2, W-4, 1099, and 941.

The period for keeping other tax records generally corresponds to the period of time that the IRS can conduct an audit and assess back taxes. In most cases, this means that tax documents such as contribution records, records substantiating business expense reimbursements, and housing allowance designations should be retained for at least three years after the income tax filing deadline for the year in question. There is no limit on how far back the IRS can assess taxes in cases of fraud, filing a false return, willfully attempting to evade tax, or failing to file a return. If there is any possibility that one of these "unlimited" assessment periods may apply, then you may want to keep relevant records permanently.

Federal and state nondiscrimination laws specify how long to keep certain records. These rules should be consulted.

One final point about church records: In 2002, Congress enacted the Sarbanes-Oxley Act.

Any document that you plan to keep permanently should be stored in a secure location. This means a locked and fireproof file cabinet, or some other suitable location.

This legislation was a response to some highly publicized financial scandals involving prominent companies. The Act contains several provisions that seek to restore investor confidence by addressing matters of corporate governance. Most of these provisions are amendments to federal securities laws. Since religious organizations are exempt from most of the provisions of these laws, they are not covered by the Act's provisions. However, there are a few provisions that are amendments to federal criminal law. Since federal criminal law contains no blanket exemption for religious organizations, churches are subject to these provisions. One of these provisions makes it a crime to knowingly alter, destroy, mutilate, cover up, falsify, or make a false entry in any record or document with the intent to obstruct or influence the proper administration of any matter within the jurisdiction of any department or agency of the United States. This new crime is a felony that can lead to a substantial fine or imprisonment of up to 20 years.

Note that persons who falsify records or documents may be liable on other grounds as well. For example, the intentional falsification of tax-forms may result in liability for civil or criminal fraud under the federal tax code. For example, assume that a pastor discovers in November of this year that the church board failed to designate a housing allowance for him. He creates a housing allowance form that he backdates to December 31 of the previous year which purports to designate a housing allowance for all of the following year.

The church is exempt from most of the provisions of the Sarbanes-Oxley Act. However, the Act makes it a crime to knowingly falsify any document with the intent to influence "the investigation or proper administration of any matter within the jurisdiction of any department or agency of the United States," and this provision contains no exemption for churches or pastors. It's possible that the pastor's falsification of the housing allowance form violates this provision, exposing him to a fine or imprisonment. But even if it doesn't, the pastor's actions may expose him to civil or criminal penalties under the tax code.

Selection and Removal of Board and Congregational Members

An overview of the legal rules that apply.

Selection of board members

The procedure for selecting board members usually is described in a church's bylaws, or sometimes in its corporate charter, and so these documents should be consulted. Board members are commonly elected by the church membership at annual business meetings of the church.

However, it's also common for the board to elect its own officers.

For example, following an annual business meeting, the newly elected board of a church meets to determine which of its members will serve as secretary, treasurer, and president. There is considerable deviation from this model in churches. The procedure for selecting board members ordinarily is defined in a church's governing documents. Board members should be familiar with this procedure and follow it accordingly.

It's important to understand that a church's charter or bylaws often prescribe qualifications that a board member must meet in order to serve. For example, it's common for bylaws to specify that candidates for the board must have attained a minimum age, or have been members of the church for a minimum length of time. Some church bylaws impose additional qualifications based on their understanding of Scripture. Again, it's important for church board members to be familiar with these qualifications so that they can be properly enforced.

This brings up a related issue—how should candidates for the board be selected? The problem here is that if nominations are permitted from the floor during a church business meeting, there may not be time to determine if a candidate meets the qualifications described in the bylaws.

For example, let's say that a church does not permit members who are divorced and remarried to serve as board members. During a membership meeting, a member nominates John to be a member of the board. No one is aware that John is divorced and remarried, and John doesn't know that this disqualifies him from consideration. John is elected, and a few weeks later the pastor learns of John's previous divorce.

This poses a terrible dilemma for the church, for it now must remove John from the board, which will cause embarrassment not only for John, but also for the pastor and board, and will lead to confusion in the congregation. Can these incidents be avoided?

A church's charter or bylaws often prescribe qualifications that a board member must meet in order to serve.

If the church bylaws permit nominations from the floor during a business meeting, then the bylaws should be amended to permit nominations from the floor *only* by members who have determined *in advance* that the person they are nominating meets all of the qualifications set forth in the church bylaws. Members should be reminded of this requirement in advance of the annual business meeting, and provided with a list of qualifications for board members. If the bylaws don't specifically permit nominations from the floor, then the board can adopt the same kind of safeguard.

Another legal rule that pertains to the selection of church board members is called *staggered voting*. Staggered voting refers to the process of selecting a portion of the board at each annual business meeting, so that you don't face the possibility of an entirely new board taking office at the same time. The problem with an all-new board is a sudden lack of continuity and experience that puts a church at a real disadvantage. Staggered voting is designed to prevent this from happening. Once again, review your church bylaws to see if only a portion of your board is elected each year. If so, you have staggered voting.

Another legal principle that pertains to the selection of board members is the filling of vacancies. It occasionally happens that a church board member moves, resigns, or dies while in office, creating a vacancy on the board. Should this vacancy be filled, and if so, how?

As a general rule, vacancies occurring on the board are filled according to a church's bylaws. Church bylaws often provide for vacancies to be filled by the remaining board members for the unexpired term of the former member. This is not always the case, however. If a vacancy occurs on your church board, be sure to review your bylaws immediately to familiarize yourself with the method for filling the vacancy.

Not all church bylaws address the filling of vacancies. In such a case, the state nonprofit corporation law under which your church is incorporated may specify a procedure for filling the vacancy. If not, or if your church is not incorporated, there is no alternative but to await the next annual meeting of the congregation or to call a special meeting for the purpose of filling the vacancy for the unexpired term—but note that if your church finds itself in this position, it may have other alternative ways to address a vacancy if it has adopted a parliamentary authority.

Removal of board members

Unfortunately, there are times when a church congregation or the board itself determines that a particular board member must be removed from office. Usually this is because the board member has violated one of the qualifications for office prescribed in the church bylaws. For example, let's say that a church's bylaws specify that a board member must not engage in specified behaviors that violate the church's understanding of Scripture, and that the church learns that a board member is engaging in one or more of these prohibited behaviors. The other board members decide that this person must be removed from office. How do they go about doing so?

The first step is to review the church's bylaws to see if there is any provision dealing with the removal of a board member. If there is such a provision, it must be followed. If the church bylaws do not address this issue, then check state nonprofit corporation law if the church is incorporated. It may contain a procedure that will guide you in the removal of the board member.

If your church is incorporated under your state nonprofit corporation law, your bylaws will almost always take precedence over the nonprofit law. Nonprofit corporation laws generally will apply to a particular issue, such as the removal of directors, only to the extent that a corporation's bylaws do not address the matter.

Church bylaws often contain vague language when describing the grounds for removing a board member. An example would be unscriptural conduct. Obviously, there may be strong disagreement about whether particular behavior is unscriptural or not. It's important to refer to a group or body that has the ultimate authority to conclusively determine such issues. For example, if your church bylaws permit board members to be removed for unscriptural conduct, or on the basis of some other vague standard, then be sure to specify that the church board, or some other specific body such as the church membership, shall have the final authority in determining whether or not such a standard has been violated. This will reduce the risk of litigation, and a civil court becoming involved in reviewing the decision of a church to remove a board member.

Selection of congregational members

Church board members should be familiar with two critical legal principles that apply to the selection of members.

If your church is incorporated under your state nonprofit corporation law, your bylaws will almost always take precedence over the nonprofit law.

First is church membership. In many churches, members are given extensive authority. They select and remove board members and ministers, authorize the purchase and sale of property, amend the bylaws, and approve budgets. So, it's important to know who the members are.

Second, you need to be familiar with the procedure for selecting members. Most churches have members, and if this is true of your church, then you as a board member should be familiar with the procedure your church has adopted for recognizing members. Ordinarily, this procedure is set forth in a church's bylaws. Often, it's the church board that is given the responsibility of admitting new members. In many churches, this process involves a membership application and a determination by the board that an applicant meets the requirements for membership specified in the church bylaws.

For example, church bylaws may impose a minimum age requirement, specify that persons must have attended the church for a minimum number of years before becoming a member, require that prospective members financially support the church, attend regularly, or set forth moral standards that must be met. It's the responsibility of the church board to be familiar with such provisions, and to be sure that persons who don't meet these criteria aren't admitted to membership.

Unfortunately, internal disputes sometimes occur within churches. The ultimate resolution of such disputes often will depend upon action of the church membership. When such disputes occur, the focus of attention often is on those persons claiming to be church members.

Disagreements often erupt at this point over the accuracy of the membership roll, so it's important for church board members to be sure that only those persons meeting the qualifications set forth in the bylaws are admitted to membership.

Removal of congregational members

There are two ways for members to be removed from the active membership roll. First, they no longer attend the church or fail to meet one or more of the qualifications for church membership.

Usually, it's the church board's responsibility to periodically review and update the membership roll to be sure that such persons' names are removed. Often this isn't done for many years, and the membership roll becomes inaccurate. This can lead to serious problems.

For example, assume that a church's bylaws require that a purchase or sale of church property be approved by two-thirds of the membership. If the membership roll contains the names of several persons who no longer attend the church or who for some other reason don't satisfy the conditions of membership, you can see the kind of problems that can occur. The same thing would be true for any other kind of action that requires a vote of the membership. The lesson is clear—church boards should periodically review and update the membership roll.

This assumes of course that the board has the authority to do so, as is true in most churches. If your church board does review the membership roll, do so well in advance of the annual membership meeting so there will be time to resolve any disagreements that may occur.

You don't want to conduct your review a day or two before the annual business meeting, since there won't be enough time for persons to challenge or object to decisions that are made.

There is a second way for members to be removed from the membership roll—through the process of discipline. Some church bylaws contain a provision authorizing the discipline or dismissal of members who engage in specified types of behavior. It's common for the church board to be authorized to conduct an investigation to determine if a member should be disciplined, and if so, what the punishment should be. The board's decision usually can be appealed to the full membership in a specially called meeting. Be sure you're familiar with the grounds for discipline set forth in your church bylaws, and understand your role in the process.

As you might expect, the discipline or dismissal of a member can be a highly charged process. Many members who are not happy with the result have sued their church, claiming that the church somehow violated their rights or failed to follow its disciplinary procedure.

It's the church board's responsibility to periodically review and update the membership roll.

The vast majority of courts have refused to resolve these disputes on the ground that they are barred from doing so by the constitutional protection of religious freedom. However, a few courts have been willing to resolve these disputes under very limited circumstances—so long as they are not required to delve into religious doctrine.

For example, a few courts have resolved lawsuits by dismissed members who claim that the body within the church that dismissed them lacked the authority to do so. To illustrate, a church board dismisses a member but the church's bylaws state that only the membership can do so. A few courts have resolved these disputes if the dismissed member claims that the church failed to follow its bylaws, and finally, a few courts have resolved these disputes if there is a disagreement over the meaning of terminology contained in the church bylaws.

To illustrate, let's say that a church's bylaws specify that a member can be dismissed for failure to attend church or make financial contributions. What does this mean? How many services does a member have to miss, or how little would a member have to contribute, to be subject to dismissal? The bylaws don't say. Some courts are willing to interpret such terminology so long as they can do so without delving into religious doctrine.

Some church bylaws contain a provision authorizing the discipline or dismissal of members who engage in specified types of behavior.

As another example, let's say that a church's bylaws permit members to be disciplined for "unscriptural conduct." Once again, what actually does this mean? Does it mean lying? Being overweight? Envious? Prideful? Obviously, such terminology can create real confusion and subjectivity. However, the courts generally will not interpret language like "unscriptural conduct" since it will require doctrinal interpretations. Church board members can make this result more certain by amending the bylaws to specify that the board or some other specified body shall have the final authority to determine the meaning of unscriptural conduct, subject to any appeal procedure set forth in the bylaws.

The point is this: You want to reduce the possibility of the civil courts interpreting standards for church membership. Review the church's bylaws to see what the grounds for discipline are. If you see language that is unclear—such as failure to attend or support the church, or unscriptural conduct—then you have two choices: either amend the bylaws to spell out exactly what you mean, or give the church board or some other group within the church the authority to make final decisions regarding the meaning of such language, subject to any appeal procedure set forth in the bylaws.

Withdrawal of church membership

Case Study. In 1989, the Oklahoma Supreme Court issued a ruling that remains the definitive analysis on the discipline of church members. *Guinn v. Church of Christ, 775 P.2d 766 (Okla. 1989).* The court reached the following conclusions:

- The discipline of *church members* (i.e., persons who have *not* withdrawn from membership) is a constitutionally protected right of churches.
- Discipline of persons who have effectively withdrawn their church membership is not a constitutionally protected activity, and churches that engage in such conduct can be sued under existing theories of tort law.

The constitutional right of a church member to withdraw from church membership is protected by the First Amendment guaranty of religious freedom *unless a member has waived that right*. A church wishing to restrict the right of disciplined members to withdraw must obtain a voluntary and knowing waiver by present and prospective members of their constitutional right to withdraw. How can this be done?

One approach would be for a church to adopt a provision in its bylaws preventing members from withdrawing if they are currently being disciplined by the church.

Obviously, the disciplinary procedure must be carefully specified in the church bylaws so there is no doubt whether the disciplinary process has been initiated with respect to a member. Most courts have held that members are "on notice" of all of the provisions in the church bylaws, and consent to be bound by them when they become members. As a result, the act of becoming a member of a church with such a provision in its bylaws may well constitute an effective waiver of a member's right to withdraw (if the disciplinary process has begun).

Four Fiduciary Duties of Church Boards

Key responsibilities every board member should meet when they serve.

One of the most misunderstood legal principles in nonprofit governance is the origin and meaning of "fiduciary duties" and their application to the officers and directors of churches and other nonprofit organizations.

> **The word "fiduciary" derives from the Latin word fiduciarius, relating to something held in trust.**

Officers and directors of churches—most commonly understood to be church board members or members of church finance committees with decision-making power—must bring intentional care and oversight to the financial affairs of their churches. Whether in the for-profit or nonprofit world, there are examples of corporations or organizations that ran aground because their officers and directors either neglected to learn the financial workings of their organizations or looked the other way—or even worse, led or aided malfeasant activities. The costs of these transgressions are substantial to the organizations, but also can prove legally and financially damaging to the individual officers and directors.

Origin and nature of fiduciary duties

The word "fiduciary" derives from the Latin word fiduciarius, relating to something held in trust. Many courts and legislatures have attempted to define the fiduciary duties of the officers and directors of nonprofit corporations. The few courts that have addressed fiduciary duties in the context of nonprofit corporations have generally defined fiduciary duties of officers and directors to include the following four duties:

1. due care;
2. prudent investing;
3. loyalty; and
4. obedience.

(1) The fiduciary duty of "due care"—in general

The officers and directors of nonprofit corporations, like their counterparts in for-profit corporations, have a fiduciary duty to exercise "due care" in the performance of their duties. In one of the most detailed descriptions of this duty, a federal district court for the District of Columbia ruled that the directors of a nonprofit corporation breached their fiduciary duty of care in managing the corporation's funds. *Stern v. Lucy Webb Hayes National Training School for Deaconesses & Missionaries, 381 F. Supp. 1003 (D.D.C. 1974)*. The corporation's finance committee had not convened in more than 11 years. Under these facts, the court concluded:

> Total abdication of [a director's] supervisory role, however, is improper .... A director who fails to acquire the information necessary to supervise ... or consistently fails even to attend the meetings ... has violated his fiduciary duty to the corporation .... A director whose failure to supervise permits negligent mismanagement by others to go unchecked has committed an independent wrong against the corporation.

The court noted that a director or officer of a nonprofit corporation "has a continuing fiduciary duty of loyalty and care in the management of the [corporation's] fiscal and investment affairs," and acts in violation of that duty if:

1. he fails, while assigned to a particular committee of the board having stated financial or investment responsibilities under the bylaws of the corporation, to use diligence in supervising and periodically inquiring into the actions of those officers, employees and outside experts to whom any duty to make day-to-day financial or investment decisions within such committee's responsibility has been assigned or delegated; or
2. he knowingly permits the [corporation] to enter into a business transaction with himself or with any corporation, partnership or association in which he holds a position as trustee, director, partner, general manager, principal officer or substantial shareholder without previously having informed all persons charged with approving that transaction of his interest or position and of any significant facts known to him indicating that the transaction might not be in the best interests of the corporation; or
3. he actively participates in, except as required by the preceding paragraph, or votes in favor of a decision by the board or any committee or subcommittee thereof to transact business with himself or with any corporation, partnership or association in which he holds a position as trustee, director, partner, general manager, principal officer, or substantial shareholder; or
4. he fails to perform his duties honestly, in good faith, and with reasonable diligence and care.

The key element of the fiduciary duty of care is the performance of one's duties as a director or officer "honestly, in good faith, and with reasonable diligence and care."

There are a number of ways that church board members can reduce the risk of liability for breaching the fiduciary duty of due care, including the following:

- Attend all of the meetings of the board and of any committees on which they serve.
- In advance of each meeting, receive an agenda of matters to be addressed during the meeting, with supporting documentation.
- In advance of each meeting, receive and thoroughly review interim financial statements and other materials that will be presented to enable them to seek clarification of any questions, irregularities, or inconsistencies at the meeting of the board.
- Affirmatively investigate and rectify any other problems or improprieties.
- Thoroughly review the corporate charter, constitution, and bylaws, and be sure copies of these documents are accessible during the meeting.
- Dissent from any board action with which they have any misgivings, and insist that their objection be recorded in the minutes of the meeting.
- According to *Robert's Rules of Order Newly Revised*: "No action of acceptance ... is required—or proper—on a financial report of the treasurer unless it is of sufficient importance, as an annual report, to be referred to auditors [in which case] it is the auditors' report which is accepted."
- Provide members with the preliminary minutes of each board meeting soon after the meeting is held, and invite additions and corrections.
- Make sure that all actions are properly authorized and recorded in the minutes.

- Make sure that all actions are consistent with the church's charter, bylaws, or other governing instruments.
- Implement a training program for new and veteran board members.
- Resign from the board if and when you are unable to fulfill these duties.
- Several recommendations made by the Freeh Commission in response to the Jerry Sandusky scandal at Penn State University are directly relevant to church boards, and include the following: (1) the church's governing documents should provide for board rotation and staggered voting; (2) board members' terms should be limited; (3) the board should be continually informed by church leadership of existing and potential legal and financial risks.
- Encourage diversity in board membership.
- Periodically review the performance of senior level church staff.

The fiduciary duty of due care was initially formulated by the courts, and was often construed as imposing on nonprofit corporate directors a duty to act with the same degree of care in the performance of their duties as a "reasonably prudent director" under similar circumstances. The "reasonable person" standard is still followed by many courts and legislatures, but in recent years has been increasingly replaced by a slightly different standard. Most notably, **section 8.30 of the revised Model Nonprofit Corporation Act**, which has been adopted by several states, provides:

> (a) Each member of the board of directors, when discharging the duties of a director, shall act:
>
> > (1) in good faith, and
> >
> > (2) in a manner the director reasonably believes to be in the best interests of the nonprofit corporation.

(b) The members of the board of directors or a committee of the board, when becoming informed in connection with their decision-making function or devoting attention to their oversight function, must discharge their duties with the care that a person in a like position would reasonably believe appropriate under similar circumstances.

(c) In discharging board or committee duties a director must disclose, or cause to be disclosed, to the other board or committee members information not already known by them but known by the director to be material to the discharge of their decision-making or oversight functions, except that disclosure is not required to the extent that the director reasonably believes that doing so would violate a duty imposed by law, a legally enforceable obligation of confidentiality, or a professional ethics rule.

(d) In discharging board or committee duties a director who does not have knowledge that makes reliance unwarranted may rely on the performance by any of the persons specified in subsection (f) (1), (3), or (4) to whom the board may have delegated, formally or informally by course of conduct, the authority or duty to perform one or more of the board's functions that are delegable under applicable law.

(e) In discharging board or committee duties, a director who does not have knowledge that makes reliance unwarranted may rely on information, opinions, reports, or statements, including financial statements and other financial data, prepared or presented by any of the persons specified in subsection (f).

(f) A director may rely, in accordance with subsection (d) or (e), on:

(1) one or more officers, employees, or volunteers of the nonprofit corporation whom the director reasonably believes to be reliable and competent in the functions performed or the

information, opinions, reports, or statements provided;

(2) legal counsel, public accountants, or other persons retained by the corporation as to matters involving skills or expertise the director reasonably believes are matters:

(i) within the particular person's professional or expert competence, or

(ii) as to which the particular person merits confidence;

(3) a committee of the board of directors of which the director is not a member if the director reasonably believes the committee merits confidence; or

(4) in the case of a corporation engaged in religious activity, religious authorities and ministers, priests, rabbis, imams, or other persons whose positions or duties the director reasonably believes justify reliance and confidence and whom the director believes to be reliable and competent in the matters presented.

(g) A director is not a trustee with respect to the nonprofit corporation or with respect to any property held or administered by the corporation, including property that may be subject to restrictions imposed by the donor or transferor of the property.

The Model Nonprofit Corporation Act reflects the trend to replace a corporate director's fiduciary duty of "due care" with a duty to act in "good faith ... in a manner the director reasonably believes to be in the best interests of the nonprofit corporation." In practical terms, there is little difference between these two standards.

"A director or officer may be liable for a violation of fiduciary duty even in the absence of bad faith or dishonesty; affirmative malfeasance is not required—mere passive negligence can be enough to breach the duty and result in liability. Similarly, a director or officer who fails to take the steps necessary to acquire a rudimentary understanding of the business and activities of the corporation may be held liable for damage resulting from that ignorance." *Fletcher Cyc. Corp. § 844.10*.

(2) The fiduciary duty of "due care"—the "prudent investor" rule

The fiduciary duty of care applies to the investment of corporate funds. However, directors are not accountable for every bad investment they make. They are not held to a standard of perfection. Rather, they are accountable only if an investment decision was not based on "the care an ordinarily prudent person in a like position would exercise under similar circumstances." The courts have been reluctant to impose liability on directors for an exercise of poor judgment. One state supreme court, in language that has been quoted by several other courts, observed:

> [There is] a presumption that in making a business decision the directors of a corporation acted on an informed basis, in good faith and in the honest belief that the action taken was in the best interests of the company. Absent an abuse of discretion, that judgment will be respected by the courts. The burden is on the party challenging the decision to establish facts rebutting the presumption.

What steps can church officers and directors take to reduce the risk of violating the fiduciary duty of due care? Consider the following:

- **Check state law.** If your church is incorporated under state law, be sure to check your state nonprofit corporation law for any provisions that address the duties of officers and directors. This information should be made available to all of the church's officers and directors.
- **Check the church's governing documents and minutes.** The governing documents (i.e., articles of incorporation or bylaws) of some churches contain restrictions on investments. Such restrictions may

also appear in the minutes of congregational or board meetings. It is essential for board members to be familiar with these restrictions and to enforce them.

- **Use an investment committee.** Many nonprofit organizations use an investment committee to make recommendations regarding the investment of funds. This can be an excellent way to reduce the liability of board members for poor investment decisions. Rather than make decisions themselves, the board appoints an investment committee that includes individuals with proven investment or financial expertise. Committee members may include stockbrokers, CPAs, attorneys, bankers, financial planners, and business leaders. Of course, the committee's recommendations ordinarily must be approved by the governing board, but by relying on the advice of experts the board is greatly reducing the risk of being liable for poor investment decisions. After all, they were relying on the advice of experts.

  KEY POINT *The Model Revised Nonprofit Corporation Act specifies that "in discharging his or her duties, a director is entitled to rely on information, opinions, reports, or statements, including financial statements and other financial data, if prepared or presented by ... persons as to matters the director reasonably believes are within the person's professional or expert competence ... ." This language provides directors with considerable protection when relying on the advice of experts on an investment committee.*

- **Investment policy.** A church congregation or board can create an investment policy to govern investment decisions. A policy can prohibit investments in specified instruments or programs.

- **Avoid speculative or risky investments.** If a proposal sounds "too good to be true," it probably is. Any scheme that promises to "double your money" in a short period of time should be viewed with extreme skepticism. It is absolutely essential that such schemes not be pursued without the thorough evaluation and recommendation of persons with financial and investment expertise.

KEY POINT *Do not rely on the "expert opinion" of persons representing the promoter of an investment scheme. Investment schemes must be reviewed by independent and objective persons having financial and investment expertise. Ideally, these persons will be members of your church, or persons within your community who have a reputation of unquestioned integrity.*

The SEC lists four common investment scams that are perpetrated on religious organizations—pyramid schemes, Ponzi schemes, Nigerian investment scams, and prime bank scams. The SEC has provided the following warning signs of fraudulent bank-related investment schemes:

> *Excessive guaranteed returns.* These schemes typically offer or guarantee spectacular returns of 20 percent to 200 percent monthly, absolutely risk free! Promises of unrealistic returns at no risk "are hallmarks of prime bank fraud."
>
> *Fictitious financial instrument.* Despite having credible-sounding names, the supposed "financial instruments" at the heart of any prime bank scheme simply do not exist. Exercise caution if you've been asked to invest in a debt obligation of the "top 100 world banks," Medium Term Bank Notes or Debentures, Standby Letters of Credit, Bank Guarantees, an offshore trading program, a roll program, bank-issued debentures, a high-yield investment program, or some variation on these descriptions. Promoters frequently claim that the offered financial instrument is issued, traded, guaranteed, or endorsed by the World Bank or an international central bank.
>
> *Extreme secrecy.* Promoters claim that transactions must be kept strictly confidential by all parties, making client refer-

ences unavailable. They may characterize the transactions as the best-kept secret in the banking industry, and assert that, if asked, bank and regulatory officials would deny knowledge of such instruments. Investors may be asked to sign nondisclosure agreements.

Exclusive opportunity. Promoters frequently claim that investment opportunities of this type are by invitation only, available to only a handful of special customers, and historically reserved for the wealthy elite.

Claims of inordinate complexity. Investment pitches frequently are vague about who is involved in the transaction or where the money is going. Promoters may try to explain away this lack of specificity by stating that the financial instruments are too technical or complex for "non-experts" to understand.

Especially watch for—and avoid—prime-bank related schemes promoted through the Internet.

It is also best to avoid investing all or a significant portion of available funds in the stock of one company, since the lack of "diversification" creates added risk. Investing in stock generally should be avoided unless investments are sufficiently diversified (for example, through conservative mutual funds) and recommended by a knowledgeable investment committee.

KEY POINT *Remember, you are investing donated funds. This is no time to be taking risks. Not only do officers and directors have a legal duty to exercise due care in the investment of church funds. Just as importantly, they have a moral duty to be prudent in their investment decisions. No officer or director wants to explain to church members at an annual business meeting how some of their contributions were lost due to poor investments.*

- **Avoid investing in companies or programs in which a board member has a personal interest.** It's critical to avoid investing in companies or programs with direct ties to a member of your board. Such investments are not always inappropriate, but they demand a higher degree of scrutiny.

KEY POINT *A church's investments should be reviewed at every board meeting. This ensures that all investments will be continuously monitored, and that necessary adjustments are made.*

- **Trustees have a higher duty.** Sometimes church board members are designated as the trustees of a charitable trust. For example, a member dies, leaving a large sum to the church for a specific purpose, and designates the church board as the trustee of the fund. Trustees are held to an even higher degree of care in the investment of trust funds than officers or directors of a corporation. However, the Revised Model Nonprofit Corporation Act specifies that "a director shall not be deemed to be a trustee with respect to the corporation or with respect to any property held or administered by the corporation, including without limit, property that may be subject to restrictions imposed by the donor or transferor of such property." In other words, a church officer or director is not automatically deemed to be a "trustee" of church funds. Officers and directors generally are held to the higher legal standard applicable to trustees only if they are designated as trustees in a legal instrument that creates a trust fund.

Church officers and directors must take steps to inform themselves about any investment decision involving church funds. They can rely on a number of safeguards, including their own research, the recommendations of an investment committee, and common sense.

The Uniform Prudent Management of Institutional Funds Act of 2006 (UPMIFA)

The Uniform Prudent Management of Institutional Funds Act (UPMIFA) has been adopted, with minor variations, in 47 states. It replaces the Uniform Management of Institutional Funds Act (UMIFA), which was adopted by most states since its inception in 1972. UPMIFA helps in clarifying the fiduciary duty of care, and in particular the "prudent investor" rule.

Section 3 of the Act specifies:

> (a) Subject to the intent of a donor expressed in a gift instrument, an institution, in managing and investing an institutional fund, shall consider the charitable purposes of the institution and the purposes of the institutional fund.
>
> (b) In addition to complying with the duty of loyalty imposed by law other than this [act], each person responsible for managing and investing an institutional fund shall manage and invest the fund in good faith and with the care an ordinarily prudent person in a like position would exercise under similar circumstances.
>
> (c) In managing and investing an institutional fund, an institution: (1) may incur only costs that are appropriate and reasonable in relation to the assets, the purposes of the institution, and the skills available to the institution; and (2) shall make a reasonable effort to verify facts relevant to the management and investment of the fund.
>
> (d) An institution may pool two or more institutional funds for purposes of management and investment.
>
> (e) Except as otherwise provided by a gift instrument, the following rules apply:

(1) In managing and investing an institutional fund, the following factors, if relevant, must be considered:

(A) general economic conditions;

(B) the possible effect of inflation or deflation;

(C) the expected tax consequences, if any, of investment decisions or strategies;

(D) the role that each investment or course of action plays within the 2 overall investment portfolio of the fund;

(E) the expected total return from income and the appreciation of investments;

(F) other resources of the institution;

(G) the needs of the institution and the fund to make distributions and to preserve capital; and

(H) an asset's special relationship or special value, if any, to the charitable purposes of the institution.

(2) Management and investment decisions about an individual asset must be made not in isolation but rather in the context of the institutional fund's portfolio of investments as a whole and as a part of an overall investment strategy having risk and return objectives reasonably suited to the fund and to the institution.

(3) Except as otherwise provided by law other than this [act], an institution may invest in any kind of property or type of investment consistent with the standards of this section.

(4) An institution shall diversify the investments of an institutional fund unless the institution reasonably determines that, because of special circumstances, the purposes of the fund are

better served without diversification.

(5) Within a reasonable time after receiving property, an institution shall make and implement decisions concerning the retention or disposition of the property or to rebalance a portfolio, in order to bring the institutional fund into compliance with the purposes, terms, distribution requirements, and other circumstances of the institution and the requirements of this [act].

(6) A person who has special skills or expertise, or is selected in reliance upon the person's representation that the person has special skills or expertise, has a duty to use those special skills or that expertise in managing and investing institutional funds.

The Act defines an "institutional fund" as "a fund held by an institution exclusively for charitable purposes." An "institution" is defined to include "a person, other than an individual, organized and operated exclusively for charitable purposes." A "charitable purpose" is defined to include "advancement of education or religion."

As a result, UPMIFA applies to virtually all funds held by a church or other charity, and is not limited to trust or endowment funds. It is therefore essential for church leaders to be familiar with its directives, which may be viewed as a clarification of the meaning of the "prudent investor."

(3) The fiduciary duty of loyalty

Directors of nonprofit corporations have a fiduciary duty of loyalty to the corporation. This duty generally requires that any transaction between the board and one of its directors be (a) fully disclosed, (b) approved by the board without the vote of the interested director, and (c) fair and reasonable to the corporation. A board member does not have to offer the church the lowest price for a product or service to discharge the duty of loyalty. All that is required is that the price be fair and reasonable to the corporation.

There are sound reasons why a church might want to do business with a member of the board at a cost that is higher than what another business may charge. To illustrate, a church board may conclude that the church will receive better quality, and customer support, by doing business with a fellow board member. Of course, this does not mean that cost is irrelevant. At some point, the price for a product or service offered by a board member may be so much higher than what is offered by competitors that it ceases to be fair and reasonable to the church. In such a case, the duty of loyalty may be violated.

The duty of loyalty also means that a board member will not usurp a corporate opportunity. This means that board members may not enter into personal transactions in which the church would have an interest. To illustrate, assume that a church needs to expand its facilities, and a five-acre tract of undeveloped land lies adjacent to the church's property. The senior pastor of the church (who is president of the church corporation) purchases the land for himself at a cost of $100,000, and later offers to sell it to the church for $250,000. Under these circumstances, the pastor likely has violated the fiduciary duty of loyalty by usurping a corporate opportunity.

(4) The fiduciary duty of obedience

Some courts have ruled that the officers and directors of nonprofit corporations have a fiduciary duty of "obedience." This duty was described by one court as follows:

> It is axiomatic that the Board of Directors is charged with the duty to ensure that the mission of the charitable corporation is carried out. This duty has been referred to as the "duty of obedience." It requires the director of a not-for-profit corporation to "be faithful to the purposes and goals of the organization," since unlike business corporations, whose ultimate objective is to make money, nonprofit corporations are defined by their specific objectives:

perpetuation of particular activities are central to the raison d'être of the organization. *Manhattan Eye, Ear & Throat Hosp. v. Spitzer, 715 N.Y.S.2d 575 (N.Y.Sup.1999).*

The duty of obedience encompasses the duty of nonprofit board members to ensure that the church:

- Is organized and operated exclusively for religious or other exempt purposes.
- Retains its exemption from state and federal taxes. This means, for example, that the church's assets do not inure to the private benefit of individuals, that the church does not engage in more than insubstantial efforts to influence legislation, and that the church and its officers and directors do not participate or intervene in any political campaign on behalf of, or in opposition to, a candidate for public office.
- Is in compliance with its constitution, bylaws, or other governing instrument.
- Is in compliance with applicable federal, state, and local laws and regulations.

One court concluded that "[t]he duty of obedience requires a director to avoid committing ... acts beyond the scope of the powers of a corporation as defined by its charter or the laws of the state of incorporation." *Batey v. Droluk, 2014 WL 1408115 (Tex. App. 2014).*

Further aspects of the duty of care in the context of compensation:

Federal tax law

In recent years, federal tax law has helped define the fiduciary of care in some important ways. A federal appeals court has noted, in this regard, that "maybe tax law has a role to play in assuring the prudent management of charities." *United Cancer Council v. Commissioner, 165 F.3d 1173 (7th Cir. 1999).*

(1) Excess benefit transactions

One of the ways this is done is the potential liability of board members of tax-exempt organizations, including churches, for excess benefits paid to "disqualified persons" (generally, officers or directors, and their relatives). This potential liability clarifies and augments the definition of the fiduciary duty of care in the context of compensation planning.

Section 501(c)(3) of the tax code exempts churches and most other religious organizations and public charities from federal income taxation. Five conditions must be met to qualify for exemption. One is that none of the organization's assets inures to the private benefit of an individual other than as reasonable compensation for services rendered. Churches and other tax-exempt organizations that pay unreasonable compensation to an employee are violating one of the requirements for exemption and are placing their exempt status in jeopardy. However, the IRS has been reluctant to revoke the tax-exempt status of charities that pay unreasonable compensation, since this remedy is harsh and punishes the entire organization rather than the individuals who benefited from the transaction. For example, should Notre Dame University lose its tax-exempt status because of the compensation it pays to its head football coach?

For many years the IRS asked Congress to provide a remedy other than outright revocation of exemption that it could use to combat excessive compensation paid by exempt organizations. In 1996, Congress responded by enacting section 4958 of the tax code. Section 4958 empowers the IRS to assess intermediate sanctions in the form of substantial excise taxes against insiders (called "disqualified persons") who benefit from an "excess benefit transaction."

Section 4958 also allows the IRS to assess excise taxes against a charity's board members who approved an excess benefit transaction. These excise taxes are called "intermediate sanctions" because they represent a remedy the IRS can apply short of revocation of a charity's exempt status. While revocation of exempt status remains an option whenever a tax-exempt organization enters into an excess benefit transaction with a disqualified person, it is less likely that the IRS will pursue this remedy now that intermediate sanctions are available.

Intermediate sanctions consist of the following three excise taxes:

1. Tax on disqualified persons

A disqualified person who benefits from an excess benefit transaction is subject to an excise tax equal to 25 percent of the amount of the excess benefit (the amount by which actual compensation exceeds the fair market value of services rendered). This tax is paid by the disqualified person directly, not by his or her employer.

2. Additional tax on disqualified persons

If the 25 percent excise tax is assessed against a disqualified person and he or she fails to correct the excess benefit within the taxable period (defined below), the IRS can assess an additional tax of 200 percent of the excess benefit. Section 4958 specifies that the disqualified person can correct the excess benefit transaction by "undoing the excess benefit to the extent possible, and taking any additional measures necessary to place the organization in a financial position not worse than that in which it would be if the disqualified person were dealing under the highest fiduciary standards." The correction must occur by the earlier of the date the IRS mails a notice informing the disqualified person that he or she owes the 25 percent tax, or the date the 25 percent tax is actually assessed.

3. Tax on organization managers

An excise tax equal to 10 percent of the excess benefit may be imposed on the participation of an organization manager in an excess benefit transaction between a tax-exempt organization and a disqualified person (see below).

Section 4958(c)(1)(A) of the tax code defines an excess benefit transaction as follows:

> The term "excess benefit transaction" means any transaction in which an economic benefit is provided by an applicable tax-exempt organization directly or indirectly to or for the use of any disqualified person if the value of the economic benefit provided exceeds the value of the consideration (including the performance of services) received for providing such benefit. For purposes of the preceding sentence, an economic benefit shall not be treated as consideration for the performance of services unless such organization clearly indicated its intent to so treat such benefit.

Stated simply, an excess benefit transaction is one in which the value of a benefit provided to an insider exceeds the value of the insider's services. The excess benefit can be an inflated salary, but it can also be any other kind of transaction that results in an excess benefit. Here are three examples:

- sale of an exempt organization's assets to an insider for less than market value,
- use of an exempt organization's property for personal purposes, and
- payment of an insider's personal expenses.

An excess benefit occurs when an exempt organization pays a benefit to an insider in excess of the value of his or her services. In other words, an excess benefit is a benefit that is paid in excess of reasonable compensation for services rendered. The income tax regulations explain the concept of reasonable compensation as follows: "The value of services is the amount that would ordinarily be paid for like services by like enterprises (whether taxable or tax-exempt) under like circumstances (i.e., reasonable compensation)."

Compensation for purposes of determining reasonableness under section 4958 includes "all economic benefits provided by a tax-exempt organization in exchange for the performance of services." These include, but are not limited to, (1) all forms of cash and non-cash compensation, including salary, fees, bonuses, severance payments, and deferred and non-cash compensation; and (2) all other compensatory benefits, whether or not included in gross income for income tax purposes, including payments to plans providing medical, dental, or life insurance; severance pay; disability benefits; and both taxable and nontaxable fringe benefits (other than fringe benefits described in section 132), including expense allowances or reimbursements (other than expense reimbursements pursuant to an accountable plan) and the economic benefit of a below-market loan.

Income tax regulations clarify that compensation is presumed to be reasonable, and a transfer of property or the right to use property is presumed to be at fair market value, if the following three conditions are satisfied:

1. the compensation arrangement or the terms of the property transfer are approved in advance by an authorized body of the tax-exempt organization composed entirely of individuals who do not have a conflict of interest with respect to the compensation arrangement or property transfer;
2. the authorized body obtained and relied upon appropriate "comparability data" prior to making its determination, as described below; and

3. the authorized body adequately documented the basis for its determination at the time it was made, as described below.

If these three requirements are met, the IRS may rebut the presumption of reasonableness if it "develops sufficient contrary evidence to rebut the ... comparability data relied upon by the authorized body." An authorized body means "the governing body (i.e., the board of directors, board of trustees, or equivalent controlling body) of the organization, a committee of the governing body ... or other parties authorized by the governing body of the organization to act on its behalf by following procedures specified by the governing body in approving compensation arrangements or property transfers."

An individual is not included in the authorized body when it is reviewing a transaction if that individual meets with other members only to answer questions and otherwise recuses himself or herself from the meeting and is not present during debate and voting on the compensation arrangement or property transfer.

A member of the authorized body does not have a conflict of interest with respect to a compensation arrangement or property transfer *only* if the member:

- is not a disqualified person participating in, or economically benefiting from, the compensation arrangement or property transfer and is not a member of the family of any such disqualified person;
- is not in an employment relationship subject to the direction or control of any disqualified person participating in, or economically benefiting from, the compensation arrangement or property transfer;
- does not receive compensation or other payments subject to approval by any disqualified person participating in, or economically benefiting from, the compensation arrangement or property transfer;

- has no material financial interest affected by the compensation arrangement or property transfer; and
- does not approve a transaction providing economic benefits to any disqualified person participating in the compensation arrangement or property transfer who in turn has approved or will approve a transaction providing economic benefits to the member.

An authorized body has appropriate data as to comparability if, given the knowledge and expertise of its members, it has sufficient information to determine whether the compensation arrangement is reasonable or the property transfer is at fair market value.

In the case of compensation, relevant information includes, but is not limited to:

- compensation levels paid by similarly situated organizations, both taxable and tax-exempt, for functionally comparable positions;
- the availability of similar services in the geographic area of the applicable tax-exempt organization;
- current compensation surveys compiled by independent firms; and
- actual written offers from similar institutions competing for the services of the disqualified person.

For organizations with annual gross receipts (including contributions) of less than $1 million reviewing compensation arrangements, the authorized body will be considered to have appropriate data as to comparability if it has data on compensation paid by three comparable organizations in the same or similar communities for similar services. An organization may calculate its annual gross receipts based on an average of its gross receipts during the three prior taxable years.

Tax on "managers"

An excise tax equal to 10 percent of the excess benefit may be imposed on the participation of an organization manager in an excess benefit transaction between a tax-exempt organization and a disqualified person. This tax, which may not exceed $20,000 with respect to any single transaction, is only imposed if the 25 percent tax is imposed on the disqualified person, the organization manager knowingly participated in the transaction, and the manager's participation was willful and not due to reasonable cause. There is also joint and several liability for this tax. A person may be liable for both the tax paid by the disqualified person and this organization manager tax in appropriate circumstances.

An organization manager is not considered to have participated in an excess benefit transaction where the manager has opposed the transaction in a manner consistent with the fulfillment of the manager's responsibilities to the organization.

A person participates in a transaction knowingly if the person has actual knowledge of sufficient facts so that, based solely upon such facts, the transaction would be an excess benefit transaction. Knowing does not mean having reason to know. The organization manager will not be considered knowing if, after full disclosure of the factual situation to an appropriate professional, the organization manager relied on a professional's reasoned written opinion on matters within the professional's expertise or if the manager relied on the fact that the requirements for the rebuttable presumption have been satisfied.

Participation by an organization manager is willful if it is voluntary, conscious, and intentional. An organization manager's participation is due to reasonable cause if the manager has exercised responsibility on behalf of the organization with ordinary business care and prudence.

Effect on tax-exempt status

The regulations caution that churches and other charities are still exposed to loss of their tax-exempt statuses if they pay excessive compensation. The fact that such compensation arrangements may trigger intermediate sanctions does not necessarily protect the organization's tax-exempt status.

Automatic excess benefit transactions

The IRS maintains that some transactions will be considered "automatic" excess benefit transactions resulting in intermediate sanctions regardless of the amount involved. Even if the amount involved in a transaction is insignificant, it still may result in intermediate sanctions. This is an important interpretation, since it exposes virtually every pastor and lay church employee to intermediate sanctions that until now had been reserved for a few highly paid CEOs. The term "excess" in effect has been removed from the concept of excess benefits.

An automatic excess benefit is any benefit paid to a disqualified person that is not reported as taxable compensation by the recipient or the employer.

(2) Liability for failing to withhold payroll taxes

Without question, the most significant federal reporting obligation of most churches is the withholding and reporting of employee income taxes and Social Security taxes. These requirements apply, in whole or in part, to almost every church, but many churches do not comply with them because of unfamiliarity. This can trigger a range of penalties.

For example, section 6672 of the Internal Revenue Code specifies that "any person required to collect, truthfully account for, and pay over any [income tax or FICA tax] who willfully fails to collect such tax, or truthfully account for and pay over such tax, or willfully attempts in any manner to evade or defeat any such tax or the payment thereof, shall, in addition to other penalties provided by law, be liable for a penalty equal to the total amount of the tax evaded, or not collected, or not accounted for and paid over."

Stated simply, this section says that if an employer has failed to collect or pay over income and employment taxes, the trust fund recovery penalty may be asserted against those determined to have been *responsible and willful* in failing to pay over the tax. Responsibility and willfulness must both be established. Many church board members will satisfy this definition, which makes them potentially liable for their church's failure to withhold payroll taxes or transmit them to the government.

The potential liability of church board members for a church's failure to withhold payroll taxes, or transmit them to the government, is an example of the use of federal tax law to compel compliance by church board members with their fiduciary duties.

(3) Private benefit

The IRS defines private benefit as follows:

> An IRC section 501(c)(3) organization's activities must be directed exclusively toward charitable, educational, religious, or other exempt purposes. Such an organization's activities may not serve the private interests of any individual or organization. Rather, beneficiaries of an organization's activities must be recognized objects of charity (such as the poor or the distressed) or the community at large (for example, through the conduct of religious services or the promotion of religion). Private benefit is different from inurement to insiders. Private benefit may occur even if the persons benefited are not insiders. Also, private benefit must be substantial in order to jeopardize tax-exempt status. *IRS Publication 1828*.

The prohibition of private benefit is an example of the use of federal tax law to compel compliance by church board members with their fiduciary duties (specifically, the duties of loyalty and obedience).

Effect of violations of fiduciary duties

Even if a breach of fiduciary duties occurs, the questions become (1) who could challenge the breach, and (2) what remedies are available? The vast majority of cases alleging breach of fiduciary duties involve shareholder "derivative" lawsuits against a for-profit corporate board for financial losses. Shareholders claim that the board's breach of fiduciary duties resulted in an undervaluation of shares for which the individual board members may be personally liable. But such cases are of limited relevance to churches and other nonprofit corporations that do not have shareholders who have experienced a direct financial loss (undervaluation of shares). Even without shareholders in a church, and the reduced likelihood of any litigation targeting board members with respect to their fiduciary duties, the bottom line is that board members should take these duties seriously and faithfully meet them throughout their service on the board.

There have been very few cases involving breaches of fiduciary duties by nonprofit board members. Churches and other nonprofit corporations typically do not have shareholders, some lack "members," donors lack standing to challenge violations of fiduciary duties, and state attorneys general who have the legal authority to investigate such breaches rarely do so. Further, uncompensated board members of nonprofit corporations have limited immunity from liability for their ordinary negligence, which may be asserted as a defense by nonprofit board members in any case alleging a violation of their fiduciary duties. These factors generally mean that it is difficult to hold board members of churches and other nonprofit corporations for breaches of their fiduciary duties. However, the personal liability of board members of churches and other nonprofit organizations may consist of one or more of the following:

- A board's authorization of excess benefits for "disqualified persons" can lead to intermediate sanction penalties against "managers" (i.e., board members) under section 4958 of the Internal Revenue Code.

- A board's authorization of unreasonable compensation may result in "inurement" of a church's assets to the personal benefit of a private individual, thereby jeopardizing a church's tax-exempt status.
- A board member's violation of fiduciary duties may result in removal from office pursuant to a church's bylaws or other governing document.
- Several state nonprofit corporation laws specify that board members are personally responsible for authorizing a loan to an officer or director that is not repaid.
- Several state nonprofit corporation laws specify that board members are personally liable for approving a transaction that violates a board member's fiduciary duty of loyalty.
- One court upheld an $8,000 verdict against a church board member based on a breach of his fiduciary duties. This illustrates that money damages may be assessed against church board members who violate their fiduciary duties. *Shepherd of the Valley Lutheran Church v. Hope Lutheran Church, 626 N.W.2d 436 (Minn. App. 2001).*

Conclusion

Officers and directors of churches are tasked with serving countless hours to help guide and lead their congregations. It can be a demanding effort, and perhaps at times, a seemingly thankless one. Understanding the fiduciary duties of the board is essential to success. It's also essential to your church's overall health and well-being. A mishandled duty can lead to financial and legal troubles for board members and the church, sapping time, energy, and resources away from other ministry priorities.

Why Churches Need a Conflict of Interest Policy

Conflicts of interest in church administration are unavoidable. If not handled appropriately, they can cause significant harm. Adopting and following a sound conflict of interest policy can help a church demonstrate excellence and integrity and, in turn, strengthen its witness for the gospel.

by **MICHAEL MARTIN**

Most churches are ill-equipped to handle conflicts of interest. This is one of the most compelling findings from a recent national survey of church governance practices conducted by the ECFA (Evangelical Council for Financial Accountability).

When asked to describe their governing board's conflict of interest oversight, nearly half (49%) of churches said they do *not* have a conflict of interest policy. One in ten churches (12%) indicated they "probably" have a conflict of interest policy but that the board has not reviewed it for a long time.

Only about one in six churches (16%) said they have a conflict of interest policy, refer to it when needed, and require the board and key staff members to annually complete a conflict of interest questionnaire related to the policy.

The importance of properly handling conflicts of interest

So, what's the big deal? Why is it critical for a church to properly handle conflicts of interest?

To answer these questions, we must start with a more basic question: What is a "conflict of interest" in the context of church administration?

There is potential for a conflict of interest when a person who is responsible for promoting the best interests of the church has a competing *personal interest*.

In other words, individuals in positions of influence at a church, such as board members and key leaders who are responsible for conducting and overseeing the church's business affairs, may occasionally find their personal interests competing with their duty to make decisions in the best interest of the church.

Two practical scenarios are:

EXAMPLE 1

First Church needs to hire additional personnel to keep pace with its growth. The board of First Church is responsible for hiring new ministry staff members. A spouse of one of the board members is being considered for a job opening.

The board member has an apparent conflict of interest between making a hiring decision in the church's best interest and promoting a personal interest (the hiring of the board member's spouse).

EXAMPLE 2

First Church is looking for insurance coverage. One of its board members is an insurance broker who has submitted a proposal to provide insurance for the church.

The board member has an apparent conflict of interest between making a business decision in the church's best interest and promoting a personal interest (the selection of the board member's insurance company).

Within this context, the importance of handling conflicts of interest with integrity becomes clear for at least two major reasons. They are:

1. Conflicts of interest can pose threats to church leaders maintaining their biblical duty of stewardship and legal duty of loyalty to the organization.
2. Even when leaders are able to overcome these potential threats in reality, often the simple appearance of a conflict of interest may be enough to impair trust in the church if not handled appropriately. "Conflicts of interest are messy and make for sensational news. When this happens, the conflicts of interest are the attention-point instead of the wonderful work your church is accomplishing with God's help," ECFA president Dan Busby says.

The solution

It is impossible to isolate a church from all potential conflicts of interest (certainly as long as *people* are leading ministries). Preventing all conflicts of interest should not be the goal. In fact, in certain cases, a transaction that involves a potential conflict of interest may actually achieve the church's best interests, financially and otherwise.

The critical point for churches is to ensure they have the appropriate procedures in place—in the form of a board-approved conflict of interest policy—to handle these situations with excellence and integrity when they occur.

While conflict of interest policies should be tailored to meet the specific needs of each church, all sound policies should do the following:

- Define conflicts of interest and explain their importance, as well as the purpose of the church's policy;
- Provide instructions for board members and key staff to follow when disclosing real and perceived conflicts (the what, when, where, how, and so on, of disclosure); and
- Provide instructions for how the governing body should proceed after receiving notice of a potential conflict (how the disclosure affects board discussion and voting, recording of meeting minutes, when individuals with conflicts should be recused from meetings, and so on).

In addition, conflict of interest policies should be accompanied by an annual disclosure statement or questionnaire, which periodically reminds leaders of the policy's existence and the need to make any required disclosures. Some organizations require board members to sign the conflict of interest policy/disclosure each year. (Sample conflict of interest policies and annual disclosure statements are available in the ECFA Church Knowledge Center.)

After adopting a sound policy, remember to follow these four steps in your church when situations arise involving a potential conflict of interest:

Step 1: Exclude. All parties with a conflict of interest (direct or indirect) should be excluded from the discussion and the vote related to approving the transaction.

Step 2: Compare. Obtain reliable comparability information regarding the terms of the transaction from appropriate independent sources, such as competitive bids, independent appraisals, or independent expert opinions.

Step 3: Determine. The board should determine that the transaction is in the best interests of the church, including determining whether the transaction could be misperceived by givers, constituents, or the public—since the transaction in many cases may be publicly disclosed.

Step 4: Document. Contemporaneously document Steps 1, 2, and 3.

The Parameters of a Church Business Meeting

Understanding the legal and procedural issues of conducting church business meetings.

The authority to manage church affairs generally is vested in the directors or trustees, and their acts are binding on the corporation only when done as a board at a legal meeting. Neither a minority nor a majority of the board has the authority to meet privately and take action binding upon the corporation.

The reason for this rule has been stated as follows:

> "The law believes that the greatest wisdom results from conference and exchange of individual views, and it is for this reason that the law requires the united wisdom of a majority of the several members of the board in determining the business of the corporation." *Trethewey v. Green River Gorge, 136 P.2d 999, 1012 (Wash. 1943).*

This rule has exceptions. For example, some state nonprofit corporation laws permit directors to take action without a meeting if they all submit written consents to a proposed action. Section 8.22 of the Revised Model Nonprofit Corporation Act permits such action unless the articles or bylaws provide otherwise. And some states permit directors to conduct meetings by conference telephone call. The entire board of directors of course can take action at a duly convened meeting to ratify an action taken by a minority or majority of the board acting separately and not in a legal meeting.

Corporate bylaws ordinarily specify that regular meetings of the directors or trustees shall occur at specified times and at a specified location. The designation in the bylaws of the time and place for regular meetings of the board generally will be considered sufficient notice of such meetings. In addition, special meetings may be convened by those officers or directors who are authorized by the bylaws to do so. The bylaws ordinarily require that notice of a special meeting be communicated to all directors at a prescribed interval before the meeting. The notice also must be in the form prescribed by the bylaws.

A meeting of the directors or trustees will not be legal unless a quorum is present. A quorum refers to that number or percentage of the total authorized number of directors that must be present in order for the board to transact business. The bylaws typically state the quorum requirements. In the absence of a bylaw provision, the number of directors constituting a quorum ordinarily will be determined by state nonprofit corporation law (for incorporated churches). In many states, a majority of the board will constitute a quorum in the absence of a bylaw or statutory provision to the contrary. Some nonprofit corporation laws specify that a quorum may not consist of less than a certain number. If vacancies in the board reduce the number of directors to less than a quorum, some statutes permit the board to meet for the purpose of filling vacancies. *Model Nonprofit Corporation Act § 19.*

Board meetings are often informal. The president of the corporation generally presides at such meetings, and the secretary keeps minutes. Actions of the board may be in the form of a resolution, although this is not necessary since it has been held that actions taken by the board and recorded in the minutes constitute corporate actions as effectively as a formal resolution. *Fletcher Cyc. Corp. § 419 (perm. ed. 2008).*

If a board meeting does not comply with the requirements in the corporation's bylaws or in state law, it will be invalid, and its actions will have no legal effect. Thus, meetings will be invalid and ineffective if notice requirements are not satisfied, unless all of the directors waive the defect in notice either verbally or implicitly by their attendance without objection at the meeting. Meetings will also be invalid if quorum requirements are not satisfied, and an action taken by the board even at a duly called meeting will be invalid if it was adopted by less than the required number of votes.

Procedural requirements

In 1863, a young engineering officer in the Union Army named Henry Martyn Robert (1837-1923) was asked to preside over a church meeting in New Bedford, Massachusetts, while recuperating from a bout of tropical fever. He agreed to do so, though he knew nothing about parliamentary procedure. It was a disaster. He later described the experience as follows: "I plunged in, trusting Providence that the assembly would behave itself. But with the plunge went the determination that I would never attend another meeting until I knew something of parliamentary law." This experience would motivate Robert to write *Robert's Rules of Order*. Since no publisher shared Robert's enthusiasm for his work, he published the book himself, limiting the first printing to 4,000 copies. This printing sold out immediately, and Robert's book soon became the most comprehensive and widely used treatise on parliamentary procedure in the world. *Robert's Rules of Order* has been revised several times over the years. The current edition is the 11th edition (2011).

Like Henry Robert, many church leaders are unfamiliar with parliamentary procedure, and "trust Providence" that church members will behave themselves during church business meetings and that all will go well. But sometimes meetings can become contentious, and ignorance of parliamentary procedure can have disastrous consequences. Church leaders need to do more than "trust Providence" in conducting business meetings. They need to be familiar with the basic rules that apply to the conduct of deliberative assemblies.

First, the procedural requirements for a church business meeting should be spelled out in a church's bylaws. So, you should be familiar with what the bylaws say. To the extent that the bylaws do not address a particular issue, then the provisions of your state nonprofit corporation law may apply—if you are incorporated under state law.

Second, you should understand the difference between an annual business meeting and a specially called business meeting. Most church bylaws call for an annual business meeting, and it is at this meeting that the important business of the church is conducted, board members are elected, the budget approved, reports presented, and in some cases the pastor elected or re-elected. A specially called business meeting on the other hand is for a specific purpose, and may be called at any time.

Third, a church must comply with notice requirements in calling a business meeting. Again, these should be set forth in your bylaws, and it's important for you to understand them and be sure they are followed. Notice simply means informing the members of the upcoming meeting. It's common for church bylaws to require notice of an annual or special meeting to be given by announcement from the pulpit during the two consecutive services preceding the scheduled meeting.

The notice requirements must be taken seriously. Some courts have struck down actions taken at annual church business meetings because the notice requirements were not strictly followed. The notice requirements for special business meetings often require that the specific purpose of the meeting be described in the notice. The idea here is that a special meeting is always prompted by some specific purpose, and this purpose should be described in the notice of the meeting so that members can decide whether or not they want to attend. A number of courts have struck down actions taken at special business meetings on the ground that the notice did not describe the purpose of the meeting. Obviously, it's important to be familiar with the notice requirements, both for general and specially called meetings, and to insure that they are strictly followed.

A fourth procedural requirement associated with church business meetings is quorum. A quorum refers to the minimum number of members that must be present in order for a valid business meeting to occur. The quorum requirement should be set forth in your church's bylaws. Many churches (and organizations generally) are too idealistic when setting their quorum threshold. Do not set it too high. The rule of thumb is the number of people you can expect to attend in inclement weather. Ten percent is generally a good number. If not, check the state nonprofit corporation law under which your church is incorporated. Be sure you're familiar with the quorum requirement, and that it's satisfied in every annual and special meeting. Failure to do so can lead to a challenge to the legal validity of all of the business that occurred during a meeting at which a quorum was not present.

Parliamentary law, a fifth procedural requirement associated with church business meetings, refers to those rules that apply in the conduct of a public meeting. There are three important considerations for church board members to note regarding parliamentary procedure. First, churches should not assume that *Robert's Rules of Order* is the only manual of parliamentary procedure. It isn't. There are dozens of alternative manuals of parliamentary procedure, some of which are excellent and even superior alternatives. Second, many churches adopted the original *Robert's Rules of Order* or one of the more recent revisions. The original text was published in 1876 and has been revised several times. Obviously, churches that select "Robert's Rules" should be sure to identify this manual of parliamentary procedure as "the most recent revision of *Robert's Rules of Order*." Otherwise, they may have to resort to obsolete rules to resolve parliamentary questions. Third, no manual of parliamentary procedure should serve as a substitute for specific provisions in a church's bylaws. In other words, the fact that a church wanting to prohibit absentee voting has adopted the latest version of *Robert's Rules of Order*, which prohibits absentee voting, shouldn't serve as substitute for a bylaw provision prohibiting such voting. There is no assurance that a civil court would regard the adoption of "Robert's Rules" as an exception to the general rule that state nonprofit corporation law will control when a church's bylaws are silent. Bylaws are (and should be) hard to change. So churches should consider placing the essentials in the bylaws, and leaving the rest to the parliamentary authority or special rules.

The civil courts have shown little reluctance in invalidating actions taken at church business meetings that were not conducted in compliance with the procedural requirements set forth in the church's bylaws. Clearly, church board members have a duty to familiarize themselves with these rules, and to be sure that they are followed in the conduct of every business meeting.

Voting requirements

A number of voting requirements apply in church business meetings, such as proxy voting. This refers to one member appointing another member to vote in his or her place at a church business meeting. What if members in your church attempt to appoint proxies to vote for them at a business meeting? How would you as a board member respond?

The first thing you need to do is review your church bylaws to see if they permit proxy voting. It's rare for church bylaws to specifically authorize this type of voting, but you will need to review the bylaws to be sure. If your bylaws don't address the issue, it's possible that the state nonprofit corporation law under which your church is incorporated may allow it. Many state nonprofit corporation laws permit proxy voting unless it's specifically prohibited in a corporation's bylaws. Obviously, this can lead to unexpected consequences when a church's bylaws do not specifically prohibit proxy voting. The point here is this—if you don't want to recognize proxy voting, then you should amend your bylaws to specifically prohibit it. If you fail to do so, you may be legally required to recognize this type of voting.

A second legal issue associated with voting is absentee voting. Does your church recognize absentee voting? What if some members inform you that they won't be able to attend your next annual business meeting, and they ask for an absentee ballot? How would you respond?

This question frequently arises among churches. After all, people are accustomed to voting by absentee ballot in local, state, and national elections, and many assume that they have the same right in church elections. Whether they do or don't have such a right will depend on the wording of your church bylaws. Some church bylaws recognize absentee voting, but others don't. If your bylaws don't permit it, then the practice shouldn't be recognized—unless mandated by the state nonprofit corporation law under which your church is incorporated. As with proxy voting, if you don't want to recognize absentee voting, then your bylaws should specifically say so. If they don't, then they need to be amended—or you may be forced to recognize this practice.

Robert's Rules of Order, Newly Revised, discourages both proxy voting and absentee voting on the ground that both practices violate the fundamental principle of parliamentary law that the right to vote should be limited to the members of an organization who are actually present at the time the vote is taken in a legal meeting. Persons who are not present miss out on the opportunity to participate in the discussion and debate of important issues. Many members change their votes because of the discussion that occurs during a business meeting. It's for this reason that some churches prohibit both proxy and absentee voting in their bylaws. If your church would like to do the same, you may need to amend your bylaws.

Case Study: Proxy Votes

During a regular church business meeting, a member moved to terminate the services of the church's minister. Of the members present, 42 voted to retain the minister, and 32 voted to remove him. In addition, one of the 32 dissidents produced a list of 57 proxy (absentee) votes to remove the minister from office. The moderator of the business meeting refused to recognize the proxy votes, and the attempt to remove the minister failed. The dissident members thereafter filed a lawsuit seeking a court order upholding the validity of proxy votes in church business meetings. A state trial court ruled against the dissidents, and the case was appealed directly to the Alaska Supreme Court.

In an important decision, the court reversed the trial court and held that the proxy votes should have been counted. It based its decision on the provisions of the Alaska Nonprofit Corporations Act (under which the church had incorporated) which authorized proxy voting by members of nonprofit corporations absent a contrary provision in an organization's charter or bylaws.

The court rejected the church's claim that requiring it to recognize proxy votes violated the constitutional guaranty of religious freedom. Finally, the court observed that a church could easily avoid the recognition of proxy votes by simply amending its charter or bylaws to so state. *Herning v. Eason, 739 P.2d 167 (Alaska 1987)*

Another legal issue associated with voting is whether voting in church business meetings should be by voice vote, a show of hands, or by secret ballot. In general, the method used is governed by the church bylaws. If the bylaws don't address this issue, then the established custom will control. The members present at a meeting can also approve of a particular manner of voting if the church bylaws do not address the issue. *Robert's Rules of Order, Newly Revised*, recommends that certain votes be by secret ballot. These include the election of officers and the discipline of a member or officer. *Robert's Rules* clarifies that a vote by secret ballot can be ordered on any motion, without debate, by a majority vote of the membership.

The percentage vote needed to adopt an action is another legal issue to consider about voting. The general rule of course is that a majority vote of those members present and voting at a duly called business meeting at which a quorum is present is all that is needed to take action. However, church bylaws sometimes impose a greater voting requirement. For example, some church bylaws require a greater percentage, such as two-thirds or three-fourths, to buy or sell property, elect a pastor, or amend certain provisions of the charter or bylaws. It's up to the church board to be familiar with all of these requirements, and the only way to do this is to be familiar with the church's charter and bylaws.

If a church takes an action by a majority vote, and it's later discovered that the bylaws required a two-thirds vote, then this will have the effect of invalidating the previous action. Obviously, this can be a very embarrassing situation that also may lead to serious legal consequences. Occasionally, a church's charter, bylaws, and, in some cases, its constitution contain conflicting provisions regarding the required number of votes necessary for a particular action. The general rule to follow here is that provisions in the charter prevail over provisions in the constitution or bylaws, and that provisions in a constitution prevail over provisions in the bylaws.

Qualified privilege

Occasionally church members make statements in the course of a business meeting about another member that may be considered defamatory. For example, a pastor mentions that a church employee was dismissed because of embezzlement or some other kind of misconduct, or a member is being disciplined for failure to live up to the church's standards. Many courts have recognized that members who make statements to other members during church business meetings are protected from liability by a qualified privilege. This means that they can't be liable for defamation unless they knew the statements they made were false or they made them with a reckless disregard as to whether they were true or false.

This is a very difficult standard to prove, meaning that church members are given a good deal of protection in sharing matters of mutual concern during membership meetings. The idea is this—the law wants to encourage the free flow of information among members. There are limits however—you can't make statements about another member that you know are false, or that you make recklessly. But short of this, the law will protect you from liability. There is one other important condition that must be emphasized here. This qualified privilege applies only to statements made by members to other members. So, if nonmembers are present during a church business meeting, then the qualified privilege will not apply. If you want the protection of the qualified privilege, then steps must be taken to ensure that nonmembers are not present.

Mastering Minutes for Church Business Meetings

Understanding what should and shouldn't be recorded in the minutes and why.

by **FRANK and ELAINE SOMMERVILLE**

Meeting minutes preserve a record of actions taken during a church meeting for future reference. However, in many churches, the duty to record the minutes becomes the responsibility of an individual with little or no training in recording meeting minutes.

This often means the minutes will be insufficient, or worse, damaging to the church. A worst-case scenario exists where meeting minutes are not kept at all, therefore jeopardizing the ability of a church to document and demonstrate its actions.

Anyone with a role that involves capturing minutes from a church business or committee meeting should receive basic information on how to record and preserve meeting minutes.

The overall goal is to create a self-contained document to provide evidence of actions taken at a properly publicized, called, and run meeting. Minutes should show the meeting was properly called and noticed, that a quorum existed at the meeting, and that all decisions were approved by the required number of votes by qualified voters attending the meeting, in person, or, if permitted, by proxy. The meeting minutes should accurately report all decisions that occurred during the meeting.

These rules apply to member meetings, meetings of the board of directors (sometimes called a board of elders, a vestry, a session, or a church council), and all committee meetings.

To accomplish this, churches should establish procedures to assist the volunteers and staff members who oversee this vital governance function. These procedures should include guidance in the following areas:

Who records the minutes?

Every state's nonprofit corporate statute requires a nonprofit corporation to have a corporate secretary. While the statute allows churches to substitute a different name, the duties of the office of secretary in a church must equal or exceed the duties contained in the statute. In some churches, the office is called "Church Clerk" or something similar. In addition, a church's bylaws may add additional duties and/or provide details about how the secretary is to perform his/her duties.

The corporate secretary must record and keep minutes from all corporate meetings. The bylaws also usually require the corporate secretary to record minutes from board and committee meetings. In some cases, an assistant secretary may be appointed to assist with these duties, or each committee is authorized to appoint its own secretary. In any instance, it is important for a church to determine if each of its governing bodies has a properly appointed person to be responsible for the minutes of its meetings.

What should the minutes contain?

Training should focus on the information the minutes must contain. The minutes should demonstrate everything that would be necessary to prove that the decisions were made at a properly called and noticed meeting, along with the actions taken. To assist in this education, the church may wish to have its secretary(ies) receive training from the church's legal counsel.

At a minimum, the minutes should contain:

1. Date, time, and place of the meeting
2. Who called the meeting
3. A copy of the notice given to the meeting participants
4. A description of those who possess voting rights at the meeting
5. The names of all who attended (both members and guests)
6. The secretary's affirmation that a quorum exists, including the number of voters present (in person or by proxy, if permitted) at the meeting and the total number of voters entitled to vote
7. The time that the presiding officer called the meeting to order
8. Approval of the last meeting minutes (as modified, if necessary)
9. The exact resolutions presented, plus any amendments
10. The name of the member introducing the resolution
11. Whether each resolution that was considered passed or failed (as modified, if applicable)
12. The names of all nominees for elected offices
13. The exact vote in each election for office
14. A copy of any written reports that were received at the meeting
15. If an oral report was received without a written report, a brief summary of the oral report

16. Adjournment or recess, including time adjourned and/or time for reconvening the meeting

What should the minutes not contain?

Many times minutes contain unnecessary information that may be harmful to the church. The minutes should not contain any discussions between members regarding matters placed before them or any details about the deliberative process that preceded decisions. The minutes should not include the contents of executive sessions, but the minutes should reflect that the members went in and out of executive session.

You can take action in executive session. The action is not a secret, only the discussion. When the group comes out of executive session, they should report the action taken.

The minutes should not contain any discussions with attorneys, certified public accountants, and insurance adjusters that may be privileged. However, minutes should include decisions made as a result of discussions with attorneys, CPAs, and adjusters.

Securing the minutes

Taking sufficient minutes won't protect the church if the minutes are not secured. It is not uncommon for minutes to be maintained by individuals and then kept by those individuals off church property. Since minutes are considered permanent documents, the church must establish how the minutes are submitted to the church so they can be secured with other permanent records of the church. If minutes are kept by individuals, then they risk being lost or inadvertently destroyed.

Minutes matter

Minutes matter. They are a record of the church's history, and often play an important role in future events. Care should be taken to maintain accurate minutes of every meeting of your church.

Electronic Participation in Church Board Meetings

Four valid grounds for electronic participation in church business meetings

Bylaws

The first place to look in evaluating the legality of board members' participation in board meetings by means of electronic communications is a church's bylaws or other governing document. While few churches address this subject in their bylaws, it is a practice that should be considered.

Nonprofit corporation law

If the participation by board members in board meetings by means of electronic devices is not authorized in a church's bylaws, is it permitted by applicable nonprofit corporation law? That depends on whether a church is incorporated and the provisions of the applicable nonprofit corporation law.

A majority of states (39) have adopted the Model Nonprofit Corporation Act or the Revised Nonprofit Corporation Act, and this has provided considerable uniformity on matters of nonprofit corporation law.

To illustrate, the Model Nonprofit Corporation Act and the Revised Model Nonprofit Corporation Act (1987 and 2008 editions) provides:

> Unless the articles or bylaws provide otherwise, a board may permit any or all directors to participate in a regular or special meeting by, or conduct the meeting through the use of, any means of communication by which all directors participating may simultaneously hear each other during the meeting. A director participating in a meeting by this means is deemed to be present in person at the meeting.

There is some variation in state nonprofit corporation laws regarding the conduct of electronic meetings. Church leaders should be familiar with the wording of their state nonprofit corporation law's treatment of electronic meetings before amending the church's bylaws to provide for such meetings.

Parliamentary procedure

The eleventh edition of *Robert's Rules of Order Newly Revised* clarifies that a church's bylaws can authorize the conduct of official meetings of members in electronic meetings "at which, rather than all participating members being physically present in one room or area as in traditional (face-to-face) meetings, some or all of them communicate with the others through electronic means such as the Internet or by telephone."

A meeting conducted by electronic means "does not lose its character as a deliberative assembly so long as the meetings provide, at a minimum, conditions of opportunity for simultaneous aural communications among all participating members equivalent to those of meetings held in one room or area. Under such conditions, an electronic meeting that is properly authorized by the bylaws is treated as though it were a meeting at which all the members who are participating are actually present."

KEY POINT *Membership meetings in most churches are too large to be conducted by electronic means. As a result, the option of electronic meetings will have the most relevance to board and committee meetings consisting of a smaller number of participants.*

Robert's Rules of Order Newly Revised stresses that electronic meetings are allowed only if authorized by an organization's bylaws. This statement is incomplete, since it omits any reference to applicable state nonprofit corporation law. Incorporated churches can provide for electronic meetings in their bylaws only if authorized by the applicable nonprofit corporation statute. In most states, nonprofit corporation laws have been revised in recent years to allow boards to meet electronically.

Robert's Rules of Order Newly Revised calls attention to an important distinction between videoconference, audio conference, and teleconference: "Various provisions for electronic meetings are possible .... Thus, if the bylaws provide for meeting by videoconference (but not merely teleconference or audio conference) the meeting must be conducted by a technology that allows all participating members to see each other, as well as to hear each other, at the same time."

Robert's Rules of Order Newly Revised recommends that organizations wanting to authorize electronic meetings of boards and committees consider addressing the following issues in either the bylaws or standing rules:

- the type of equipment required for participation in meetings;
- contingencies for technical difficulties or malfunctions;
- determination of a quorum;
- how to raise a point of order challenging the continuing existence of a quorum;
- how to seek recognition and obtain the floor;

- how motions are to be submitted in writing;
- methods for taking and verifying votes;
- provisions for ensuring that nonmembers do not participate, especially in the case of special meetings in which confidential information will be shared.

> **KEY POINT** *Note that secret ballots generally are not possible in electronic meetings, which may make such meetings inadvisable in some cases.*

Robert's Rules of Order Newly Revised clarifies that notice of regular meetings of organizations or boards may be sent by electronic communication if a recipient has agreed to receive this form of notice. It states: "When notice is required to be sent, unless a different standard is specified that requirement is met if written notice is sent to each member either: (a) by postal mail to the member's last known address; or (b) by a form of electronic communication, such as email or fax, by which the member has agreed to receive notice."

> **KEY POINT** *Church bylaws often specify that notice of a regular or annual meeting of church members is given in one or more worship services preceding the date of the meeting. Electronic notice in such circumstances would not be allowed. However, it would be feasible for church bylaws to authorize notice of board meetings to be given in this manner.*

Established custom

In the rare event that the issue of electronic participation in church board meetings is not addressed in a church's governing documents or the state nonprofit corporation law under which a church is incorporated, then it is possible for such a practice to be authorized by established custom. Note, however, that custom in this context does not refer to sporadic or occasional examples. Rather, it means a consistent practice over a prolonged period of time.

Summary

The participation of members in board meetings by means of conference telephone or other electronic technology is permissible if authorized by a church's bylaws or other governing document, the nonprofit corporation law under which a church is incorporated, *Robert's Rules of Order Newly Revised* or other parliamentary authority, or established custom. If participation by board members in church board meetings is not validated by any of these methods, then the legal status of any actions taken in meetings may be jeopardized. This is more likely if the applicable quorum requirement was not met by persons in physical attendance at the meeting or there is a question regarding the number of people favoring or opposing a motion.

The simplest way to authorize participation in church board meetings by conference telephone call or other electronic means is to include a provision in a church's bylaws or other governing document that authorizes the practice. As with any bylaw amendment, the assistance of an attorney is recommended.

Here are the key elements to include:

- A provision stating that a board member can "attend" a regular or special meeting of the board by conference telephone call or other electronic device;
- A general definition of the technology allowed;
- A stipulation that the approved electronic technology must allow each participant in the meeting to hear and be heard by the other participants at the same time;

- A note that a person is "present" if using approved electronic equipment, and is counted in determining if a quorum exists.

How should church leaders determine the governing document to apply when there is a conflict in the various sources of authority? Table 2 in the Appendix provides church leaders with a tool for determining the ranking of various sources of authority in "congregational" churches (those that function independent of a religious hierarchy).

Preparing for the Annual Business Meeting

A 15-point checklist to help you prepare for the annual meeting.

Most churches conduct an annual business meeting for members. Many churches use the annual business meeting to elect board members, adopt a budget, approve reports, authorize the purchase or sale of church property, and discuss new items of business. As a church leader, you should be familiar with a number of issues that may arise in your annual church business meeting.

1. Current copy of church bylaws. As hard as it may be to believe, many church leaders cannot identify the current version of their church's governing document (which we will refer to as the "bylaws"). Often there are multiple versions in circulation. Usually, this occurs because older versions not incorporating the most recent amendments are still being used. Prior to the annual business meeting the church board should identify the current version and have a copy available at the meeting. This official version should be prominently dated (as of the most recent amendment) at the top of the cover page. A chronology of all amendments to the bylaws can be prepared by reviewing the minutes of all annual and special meetings. This chronology will enable church leaders to quickly identify obsolete versions of the bylaws. These versions should be archived for posterity and continuity as church leadership changes. But leaders will want to make certain any old retained versions are clearly labeled with the dates they were in effect.

2. Reviewing the membership list. Check the church bylaws to see what they say about the identification of church members. It is common for church bylaws to call for a periodic review of the membership list so that the names of persons who fail to meet specified conditions can be removed. For example, it is common for church bylaws to limit members to persons who regularly attend or support the church. In such a case it is important for the church's membership standard to be properly and consistently applied. This is a task that should be done annually, pursuant to the process spelled out in the bylaws. Many church boards neglect this duty, and this often compounds the problem of deciding who active voting members in good standing are.

3. Prescreening candidates for the church board. Many churches have bylaws that prescribe various qualifications for members of the board. This can present problems if members are allowed to make nominations from the floor during an annual business meeting. If your church bylaws contain a list of qualifications for members of the board, and board members are elected at annual business meetings, then it is a good practice for the church board to appoint a nominating committee that prescreens and selects a list of candidates who meet those qualifications. Members should be advised during the membership meeting not to make additional nominations from the floor unless they have determined in advance that their nominee meets the qualifications specified in the bylaws.

4. Notice. The church membership ordinarily must be notified of the date, time, and place of annual membership meetings. In the case of a special meeting, the notice generally must state the purpose of the meeting (in addition to the date, time, and place). The "notice" requirements usually are found in a church's bylaws, but also may appear in the corporate charter or in the body of parliamentary procedure adopted by the church. If a church is incorporated and its bylaws do not address notice requirements, the state nonprofit corporation law ordinarily will contain the applicable requirements. Unincorporated churches that have no bylaws or written regulations are bound by their established customs regarding notice of church membership meetings. A church must comply with the manner and method of giving notice prescribed in the bylaws. Failure to follow such requirements may render any action taken at the meeting invalid. However, a number of courts have ruled that members must object to defective notice at the meeting in question, and that a failure to do so will constitute a "ratification" of the defective notice.

5. Quorum. A "quorum" refers to the minimum number of members who must be present at an annual or special business meeting in order for business to be transacted. This number usually is specified in a church's bylaws. If it is not, then state nonprofit corporation law will specify a quorum if the church is incorporated. It is important for church board members to know the applicable quorum requirement.

6. Voting majorities. Often there is confusion regarding the number of votes required to adopt a particular action. For example, if the church bylaws require a particular vote to be by "a majority of members," does this mean a majority of the total church membership or a majority of those members present at a duly convened membership meeting? A church can and should define the term *majority of members* to avoid this confusion. But if a church's bylaws nowhere define *majority of members*, or any other term relating to the required number of votes needed to adopt an action, the fraction or percentage of votes needed to adopt an action generally refers to the members present and voting at a duly called meeting and not to the entire church membership. If a church's bylaws do not designate the required percentage of votes for an affirmative action, then there is a presumption of majority rule. Church bylaws may impose a higher voting requirement than a simple majority for some actions. Common examples are the purchase or sale of real estate, and voting for a pastor. Board members should be familiar with all of the voting requirements specified in the bylaws to be sure that official actions are taken with the legally required number of votes.

7. Absentee ballots. Absentee voting is not ordinarily permitted unless specifically authorized by a church's bylaws or by statute. *Robert's Rules of Order* specifies: "An organization should never adopt a bylaw permitting a question to be decided by a voting procedure in which the votes of persons who attend a meeting are counted together with ballots mailed in by absentees, since in practice such a procedure is likely to be unfair."

8. Proxy voting. Proxy voting refers to voting by means of a substitute. For example, a church member appoints another member to vote on his behalf at a membership meeting that he cannot attend. Churches rarely intend to permit proxy voting. *Robert's Rules of Order* specifically discourages it. Few, if any, state nonprofit corporation laws require proxy voting, but some states permit it unless specifically repudiated in an incorporated church's bylaws. Incorporated churches not wanting to recognize proxy voting should review their bylaws to determine if they contain a provision prohibiting it. If not, an amendment would be in order. It should not be assumed that a church's formal adoption of *Robert's Rules of Order* will result in the prohibition of proxy voting.

9. Other methods of voting (by hand, secret ballot, absentee voting). Votes can be cast orally, by show of hands, or by secret ballot. The method used is governed by the church's bylaws. If these documents are silent, established church custom will control. The members present at a meeting can also approve of a particular manner of voting if the church's bylaws do not address the subject.

10. Parliamentary committee. The church board should designate a parliamentary committee to serve during the annual business meeting. If the church's bylaws do not adopt a particular body of parliamentary procedure (there are several), they should be amended to do so. Church leaders should never assume that *Robert's Rules of Order* automatically applies. It doesn't. Once a church adopts a particular body of parliamentary procedure, leaders should note that they may wish to adopt special rules that outline a specific discipline process or dissolution procedure. When special rules are adopted, they fall below church bylaws in the hierarchy.

11. Financial reports and audits. Be sure to review the church's bylaws to see what kinds of reports must be presented at the annual business meeting. To illustrate, some church bylaws require an annual audit and a presentation of the audit at the annual business meeting. Be sure the church complies fully with such a requirement. Note that the word "audit" has a specific meaning. It does not include various "limited engagements" that CPAs can perform. If your bylaws call for an audit, be sure that the financial report that you present in your annual membership meeting is in compliance with your church bylaws.

12. Amendment requirements. Can the bylaws be amended in the course of an annual business meeting? Some church bylaws permit this to be done. However, it also is common for church bylaws to require advance notice of any proposed bylaw amendment, and this prevents members from proposing and enacting bylaw amendments during an annual business meeting. Church board members must be familiar with the amendment provision in the church bylaws.

13. Procedure. Be sure to follow any other procedural requirements that are spelled out in the church bylaws. These may include the appointment of a recording secretary, the presentation and approval of a church budget, and a specified order of business.

14. Disclosure of salary information. Some churches disclose the salaries paid to staff members, while others do not. If your church does not disclose this information, you should be prepared to respond to a member who asks for this information during the annual business meeting. Some churches that do not disclose salary information will inform the congregation that all salaries are within the average ranges of compensation paid by other churches of the same size for similar positions (if such is the case).

15. Resolving conflicts in a church's organizational documents. What if there are conflicting provisions in a church's charter and bylaws (or other governing document) regarding the required number of votes necessary for adoption of a particular action? In general, provisions in the charter prevail over provisions in a church's constitution, bylaws, or resolutions; provisions in the constitution prevail over provisions in the bylaws, or resolutions; and provisions in the bylaws prevail over provisions in resolutions. In most cases, an incorporated church is bound by the provisions of state nonprofit corporation law only where it has not expressly provided otherwise in its own charter, constitution, bylaws, or parliamentary authority.

Appendix

Common Sources of Parliamentary Procedure

While ***Robert's Rules of Order (11th ed. 2011)*** is by far the most widely used parliamentary authority, other authorities exist. These include:

(1) Demeter's Manual of Parliamentary Law and Procedure (1969) is shorter than *Robert's Rules* but not widely used. An interesting feature is a final chapter on "The Greatest Convention Ever Held," which contains an account of the biblical Creation. The 1969 edition is a revision of the original 1953 work.

(2) Riddick's Rules of Procedure (1985). The work of Floyd Riddick, former parliamentarian of the United States Senate. His work consists of an alphabetical list of parliamentary phrases rather than a systematic body of parliamentary procedure, and is of little use to persons with limited familiarity with parliamentary procedure.

(3) American Institute of Parliamentarians Standard Code of Parliamentary Procedure. A parliamentary authority written by Alice Sturgis in 1950. The current edition (2012) was written by the American Institute of Parliamentarians. Its main objective is to provide a parliamentary authority that is simpler and more up-to-date than *Robert's Rules*. Its cover contains the following quote from former American Institute of

Parliamentarians president Leo Athans: "Anyone who has trouble with *Robert's Rules of Order* will welcome the simplicity of this streamlined guide to parliamentary procedure." *The Standard Code of Parliamentary Procedure* is the second most widely used parliamentary authority in the United States.

Table 1: Provisions Commonly Found in Governing Documents

Charter	Constitution	Bylaws	Resolutions
Name Address Duration Purposes Names and addresses of initial board members Dissolution clause	[many churches only use bylaws, and not bylaws plus a constitution; this column assumes that a church has both documents] doctrinal tenets (and any other matter whose amendment is subject to a greater voting requirement)	• qualifications, selection, and discipline of members • time and place of annual business meetings • calling of special business meetings • notice for annual and special meetings • quorum • voting rights • selection, tenure, and removal of officers and directors • filling of vacancies • responsibilities of directors and officers • method of amending bylaws • purchase and conveyance of property • adoption of a specific body of parliamentary procedure • a clause requiring disputes between church members, or between a member and the church itself, to be resolved through mediation or arbitration	housing allowances for clergy accountable business expense reimbursement arrangement clergy compensation package

Charter	Constitution	Bylaws	Resolutions
		• a clause specifying how contracts and other legal documents are to be approved and signed • signature authority on checks • "bonding" of officers and employees who handle church funds • an annual audit by independent certified public accountants • an indemnification clause • specification of the church's fiscal year • "staggered voting" of directors (a portion of the board is elected each year-to ensure year-to-year continuity of leadership)	

Table 2: Priority among Governing Documents in Congregational Churches

NOTE: When attempting to resolve any question of church administration in a "congregational" church (a church that functions independent of a religious hierarchy), relevant provisions in the following sources of authority generally are applied in the following order of priority.

Document	Order of priority
charter	• the highest order of priority • its provisions take priority over any other source of authority • start with the charter when attempting to resolve a question of administration; if it doesn't address the matter, then proceed on to the next order of priority until an answer is found

Document	Order of priority
constitution	• the second-highest order of priority • takes priority over all other sources of authority except the charter, assuming that it is made superior to the bylaws either by express provision or by a greater voting requirement to amend
bylaws	• the third-highest order of priority • takes priority over all other sources of authority except the charter and constitution (assuming the constitution is made superior to the bylaws)
state non-profit corporation law	• the fourth-highest order of priority • its provisions generally apply only if the church has not provided otherwise in its charter, constitution, or bylaws (including rules of parliamentary law adopted by the bylaws) • state nonprofit corporation laws ordinarily make a few provisions mandatory despite a bylaw or charter provision to the contrary
resolutions	• the fifth-highest order of priority • resolutions can provide guidance in the event that the charter, constitution, bylaws, parliamentary law, and applicable state nonprofit corporation law do not address an issue
parliamentary law	• the sixth-highest order of priority (assuming that a specific body of parliamentary law has been adopted)

About the Authors

Richard R. Hammar is an attorney, CPA, and best-selling author specializing in legal and tax issues for churches and clergy. A graduate of Harvard Law School, he is the author of more than 100 books, including *Pastor, Church & Law* and the annual *Church & Clergy Tax Guide*. He also has contributed articles to numerous journals and publications, is a frequent speaker at legal and tax conferences, and has taught church law at a number of seminaries.

Michael Martin is vice president of ECFA, an organization that certifies churches and ministries for financial integrity.

Elaine L. Sommerville is a CPA and has worked in public accounting for 25 years, primarily focusing on tax compliance aspects of nonprofit organizations. She is currently the sole shareholder of the firm of Sommerville & Associates, P.C.

Frank Sommerville is a shareholder in the law firm of Weycer, Kaplan, Pulaski & Zuber, P.C. in Houston and Dallas, Texas. He also holds a license as a certified public accountant.

Both Elaine and Frank serve as editorial advisors for Church Law & Tax.

Resources

Online Resources

ChurchLawAndTax.com provides comprehensive, searchable, and easily-accessible information on legal, tax, financial, and risk management matters affecting churches and clergy. The full archives of both *Church Law & Tax Report* and *Church Finance Today* reside on the site as does the Richard R. Hammar Legal Library.

Books and Other Resources

ChurchLawAndTaxStore.com

Church & Clergy Tax Guide

Find comprehensive help understanding United States tax laws as they relate to pastors and churches with Richard Hammar's annual *Church & Clergy Tax Guide.* Tax law in general is highly complex and ever changing. Add to that the many unique rules that apply to church and clergy and you're set up for a challenging task that requires an expert's guidance.

Church Finance: The Complete Guide to Managing Ministry Resources

Overseeing the financial health of a church is no simple task. Increased regulations, IRS audits, and changing technology are a few of the challenges facing both new and experienced treasurers, bookkeepers, business administrators, and executive pastors. *Church Finance*, the groundbreaking comprehensive guide created by respected expert and CPA, Michael E. Batts gives you the confidence you need to manage every aspect of your job.

Made in the USA
Monee, IL
19 June 2024